茶經

茶經序

四之器

五之煮

六之飲

5000 years of tea

A PICTORIAL COMPANION

© 1982 CFW Publications Limited

Published by
CFW Publications Limited
130 Connaught Road Central, Hong Kong

Design:
Alan Chan

ISBN: 962 7031 24 0

Printed in Hong Kong

5000 years of tea

A PICTORIAL COMPANION

By Derek Maitland
Recipes by Jacki Passmore

Contents

Tea goes back so far in China that its origins actually lie in the depths of prehistory, in events that took place during the dawning of the oldest of the world's continuing civilisations.

Even then, the starting point is not so much documented history as what the Chinese have traditionally believed to be tea drinking's beginnings.

The most generally accepted stories involve the near super-human Emperor Shen Nung, said to have ruled China in the 28th century BC, a legendary, very likely mythical, philosopher and herbalist, also known as the Divine Husbandman. A heavenly dragon was supposedly presiding when he was born to a princess, and the dragon watched over his reign. Shen Nung is believed to have invented the plough and taught new farming techniques to his people. Lu Yu, author of the world's most famous and widely followed book on tea, the 8th century AD *Ch'a Ching*, variously translated as *The Tea Classic* or "The Tea Bible," says: "Now tea, used as a drink, was first discovered by the Emperor Shen Nung." The date of the discovery, by tradition, is 2,737 BC.

In one version, Shen Nung was watching a kettle in which water was boiling for his supper when leaves from a camellia plant, closely related to the tea plant which is also known in international nomenclature as *Camellia sinensis* or *Camellia thea*, were blown by a breeze into the kettle. In other versions it was leaves from an actual tea plant (which grew wild in China) that fell into the kettle. In any case, Shen Nung liked the aroma, sampled the infusion and

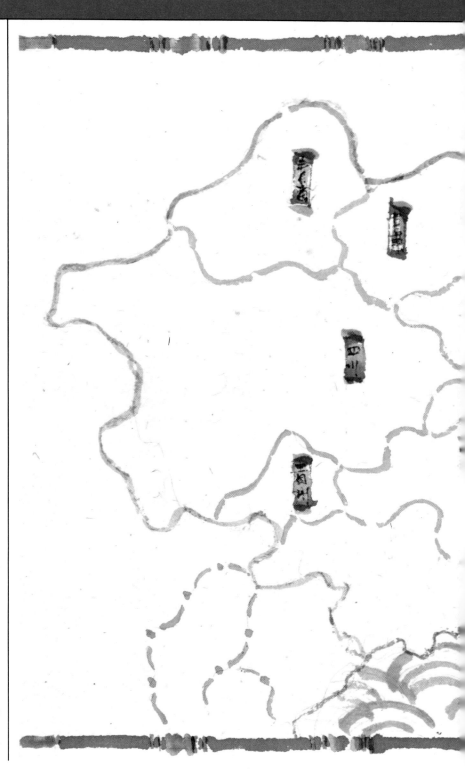

enjoyed the brew even more, and thought its joys should be shared. So he is credited with giving tea, as well as farming methods and a wide range of medicinal cures, to his people. He is supposed to have gone so far as to write a treatise on the subject of tea, lost to antiquity, in which, according to Lu Yu, he makes the point, subscribed to by all tea-lovers, that "Tea gives one vigour of body, contentment of mind, and determination of purpose, when taken over a long period of time." He supposedly added: "Better to drink such a beverage than to drink wine which loosens the tongue;"and he pointed to various medicinal benefits of tea, which even today are an integral part of Chinese tea drinking, just as they are of Chinese cuisine. He added the argument, never lost on the Chinese who seem to thrive in any climate, that drinking boiled tea has obvious advantages over possibly "infectious" water, a point well taken by the British and Europeans many centuries later, when to drink water was to flirt with disease.

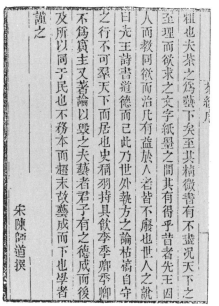

A page from the original *Ch'a Ching* (Tea Bible) and (below) a Yuan dynasty scene depicting tea vendors offering cups of tea to passers by.

Shen Nung's story may be the most widely accepted one associated with the origins of tea, but there is another very different story, widely believed in the Far East, that ties the invention of tea drinking to the spread of Buddhism, and places its origin much later, certainly later than the real facts permit. This collection of tales involves Bodhidharma, or Ta Mo, a blue-eyed Indian prince who converted to Buddhism, becoming a Buddhist saint, and went to China to enlighten its people about his religion. Regarded as the chief of the Six Patriarchs of Buddhism, he is supposed to have reached China in 526 AD. Some Asians identify him with St Thomas the Apostle. Bodhidharma believed outward observances were unimportant; he subscribed to the doctrine that perfection would come through inward meditation. But, as is the case with Christian saints, beliefs about Bodhidharma are tied up with miraculous events. One of these events, his crossing of the great Yangtze river — which divides North China from South China — on a reed is the subject of numerous sculptures and paintings. Another of his miracles involves the divine creation of tea.

For many years Bodhidharma prayed and meditated without sleep. At one point during his travels in China — the date generally given is 542 AD — he inadvertently fell asleep in Shao-lin Temple in Loyang in what is now Honan Province while meditating. When he awoke he was intensely chagrined, so disgusted in fact that he cut off his eyelids and threw them away. He then continued his meditations for five more years without sleep. When at last he did fall asleep again, upon awakening he chewed some leaves from a nearby shrub and found himself feeling alert — obviously the precious effect of the caffeine that is contained in tea. A more common and more extreme version of the story has it that when he cut off his eyelids, he threw them to the ground, they immediately took root, and the world's first tea plants grew from them. In all versions tea emerges as the symbol of eternal wakefulness.

The connection between tea and religion in old China is extensive. Ancient Chinese historians writing about the best water to use for tea constantly mention springs that happened to bubble near Buddhist temples. Followers of Taoism, China's indigenous and much older mystical system, were among the first to make tea into a popular beverage, and they looked upon it as an element in what they called the elixir of immortality. To Taoists, the wasting of a superior tea was considered, along with the false education of young people and the ignorant admiration of paintings, one of the three most deplorable acts a man could commit! Tea as an offering to gods or ancestors is part of a variety of old ceremonies that, discouraged as they are on the mainland today, are practised in most other parts of the world where Chinese congregate, especially such non-communist Chinese centres as Hong Kong, Singapore and Taiwan.

In recent years scholars have built up a considerable body of evidence that tea drinking in real fact, as opposed to myth, certainly started in China — not necessarily 5,000 years ago, but still much earlier than they had first suspected. Questions about the real origins and spread of tea drinking are tied to the use of the character *t'u* which, except for one stroke, is the same as the character *ch'a* that stands precisely for tea. In ancient writings, *t'u* has many meanings — "sow-thistle" and "smart-weed," for instance. There are references such as "The girls were like flowering *t'u*," and "the overseer is responsible for gathering ripened *t'u* for use in funeral ceremonies." One indication that *t'u* was definitely used to denote tea comes in the ancient *Book of Songs*: "Who says that the *t'u* is bitter? It is as sweet as the shepherd's purse." Many of the old scholars defined *t'u* as a bitter herb.

The evidence is unending. What is important is that scholars now generally believe, though they cannot pinpoint an exact

One school of thought links the birth of tea drinking with the arrival of Buddhism in China.

date for its beginnings, that tea drinking was fairly common in China, starting in what is now the western province of Szechuan, by at least the 6th century BC. Tea was certainly known as a beverage at the time of Confucius (about 551-479 BC), for it is discussed in the writings of one of his contemporaries, the philosopher Yen Ying. Apparently its popularity grew rapidly in the Han Dynasty (206 BC - 221 AD), when China became consolidated as a cohesive empire. The Han Emperor An Ti, incidentally, defined *ming* as buds taken from the plant *t'u*, which by now certainly meant tea. It was during this time that a stroke was dropped from the character *t'u* to form the new character *ch'a*.

By the time of the 7th century Emperor T'ai Tsung, there appeared a custom that lasted into the final dynasty of Imperial China, that of paying the Emperor a yearly tribute of tea — a practice perhaps comparable to the much later tradition of English tea merchants creating their finest blends specifically for "Royal Appointment." By the 8th century, when Lu Yu wrote his tea classic, the hard evidence of language indicated that the use of tea — which by now was also

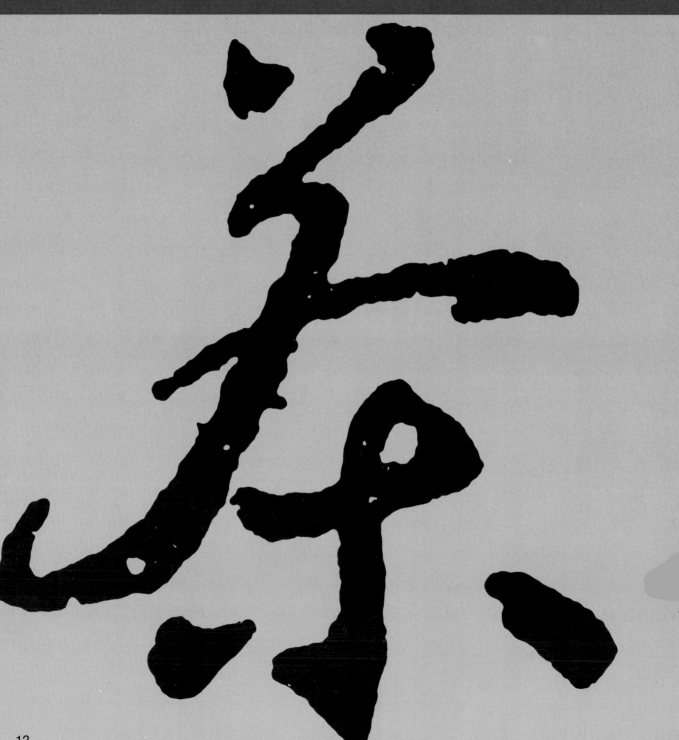

Various forms of the Chinese
character for tea.

going under the exalted synonym of "Jade Queen" — had definitely been familiar to the Chinese for at least 1,500 years.

Lu Yu himself pays homage not just to legend and the mythical Shen Nung but also to more contemporary tea drinkers like the Confucianist Yen Ying. To Lu and his followers tea drinking had become an activity worthy of a cult. One mundane story has it that a group of tea merchants commissioned him to write the *Ch'a Ching*. A more common and far more lyrical belief is that he wrote it just after walking in the wilderness chanting a poem about a fallen tree that had moved him to tears. Originally from Ching Ling in the southern Hupei Province, he was also called The Scholar of Ching Ling, and liked to present himself as The Old Gentleman of *Sang Chu* (mulberries and hemp). It is believed he was born in the second quarter of the 8th century, and lived for a time in seclusion in Chekiang Province. Judging by his writings, there is no doubt that there was, from the start, a near-religious aspect to the cult of tea-drinking that he promoted and led.

His *Ch'a Ching* sums up virtually all that was known about tea by his time, the latter part of the T'ang Dynasty (618 - 907 AD), by which time tea had become China's universal drink. Much of the *Ch'a Ching's* advice about preparation, equipage, the ways and reasons for drinking tea, the etiquette involved, are still followed. The *Ch'a Ching* is indeed a kind of tea-tippler's bible.

That Lu Yu was a man of the South is not surprising, since South China, with its startling, mist-enshrouded mountains, rivers and lakes, was not only the centre of the original tea-growing industry, but was particularly conducive to artistic and mystical endeavors. He exhalted what he called "purple" tea, the black (more accurately described by the Chinese today as red) teas that are still favoured by southerners. Black tea is a robust drink, in keeping with the spirit of the age in which he lived.

The T'ang Dynasty was an era in which the people were as robust as the kinds of tea they enjoyed, a time when daring horsemen were celebrated, a time of heroic deeds. The lusty T'ang warriors extended China's frontiers to make the Celestial Empire vaster than it had ever been before.

The favoured T'ang method for preparing tea leaves was in brick form, though other forms were already in use. When the harvest was over, the leaves were thoroughly pounded to bring out the strongest of their aromas and flavours, then shaped and pressed into special moulds, dried in special sheds over burning hardwood or charcoal, and carried on foot to the farthest reaches of the land. Brick tea later gave way to other more subtle forms of preliminary preparation, but was still to be found in China in the 19th century — and gained immense popularity in Russia where the society, like that of the Chinese, comprised a vast bulk of peasantry, topped with an icing of aristocracy, with very little in the way of a genteel, refining middle class in between.

Yet Lu Yu stressed that tea in his own time was also, and primarily so, considered a delicate brew — always to be sipped and savoured slowly, never gulped down as an instant cure for frayed nerves in the British fashion, and of course never to be served with adulterants. In Lu Yu's time every worldly phenomenon was of the utmost importance, and worthy of the greatest respect. And the act of drinking tea itself was a masterpiece of life, a moment that summed up all moments of tea drinking, as if the moment had not existed before and might not exist again. It was part of the Chinese, especially T'ang Chinese, relish for living — perhaps best illustrated by the fact that whereas to the Indians reincarnation was something frightening and to be avoided, to the Chinese the idea was highly enticing, for it meant the possibility of yet another fascinating ride on the wheel of life.

men roll tea leaves by hand in a nineteenth century Chinese processing plant.

Lu was exacting in the rules he codified for tea drinkers. "For exquisite freshness and vibrant fragrance," he said, "limit the number of cups to three. If one can be satisfied with less than perfection, five are permissible." One ancient Chinese poet was somewhat more liberal when he spoke of amounts to be drunk:

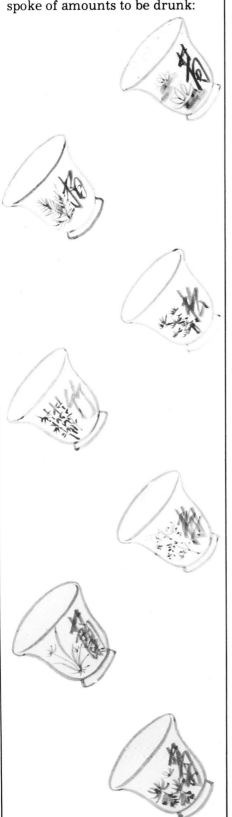

"The first cup moistens my lips...
The second cup breaks my loneliness
The third cup searches my barren entrail
The fourth cup raises a slight perspiration
The fifth cup purifies me
The sixth cup calls me to the realm of the immortals
The seventh... I can take no more."

Another old Chinese summary tells of the benefits of drinking tea throughout the day: "One cup in the morning will set the spirit stirring, refreshed, and bring the opening of untapped thoughts; one cup of tea after a meal will clear mouth odours and drive worries away; one cup of tea when you are busy will quench your thirst, drive cares away and render a feeling of tranquillity; one cup of tea after your day is done will make your bones and muscles feel lighter and dissolve your fatigue; tea will drive the doctor away, and make you feel strong; tea will add to your years, and the enjoyment of your longevity."

Indeed, both tea from the actual tea plant and tea from various other shrubs and herbs, even tree bark , is to this day considered a key to good health not only in China but around the world. It was, however, how tea affected the spirit that was of prime concern to Lu Yu and other Chinese writers down to modern times. They continually reiterate that tea should be drunk only in an atmosphere of tranquillity and for purposes of creating still greater tranquillity to better the spirit and aid in meditation — the uniquely Chinese approach.

During the Sung Dynasty (960 - 1280 AD) — the time of the greatest refinement and flowering of Chinese society and culture — brick tea gave way to powdered tea in popularity. The names of the powdered teas, which were whipped into a delicate froth — "Grey Eyebrows," "Falcon's Talon," "Ear of Corn," "Sparrow's Tongue" — are indicative of the lyrical spirit of the age. Increasingly threatened by barbarian raiders, the gentlemen of the Sung dynasty retreated into an artistic and romantic world. Their delicate tastes required an especially subtle drink.

Tea drinking went into decline for a period of less than a century which is extremely short in the Chinese reckoning of time, after the conquest of China by the northern Mongols. During the years of their Yuan Dynasty (1280 - 1368) tea and the supposed over-refined decadence that went with it were discouraged. But when the Yuan Dynasty was replaced with the vital, native Ming Dynasty (1368 - 1644) there was a tremendous revival in all things uniquely Chinese, a conscious effort to do everything — whether it be landscape painting or governing with perfection under the old Confucian system — better than it had ever been done before. And it was at this time that tea drinking not only reached new heights of refinement but also began to take on its present-day form. Just as the brick tea of the T'ang had given way to the powdered tea of the Sung, now powdered tea gave way in popularity to brewing by steeping the cured leaves. The Ming, who were an inward-looking people in spite of the exuberant artistic explosion that took place in their time, sought their inner strength from exotic outward show. They would go to extraordinary lengths to see that the very finest tea wound up in the Imperial Court — perhaps best illustrated by some of the many stories concerning the use of monkeys to collect tea leaves in Ming times.

In a light vein, there is a tale told by the renowned painter Ran In-ting that certain Buddhist monks indulged heavily in both tea drinking and opium smoking. Monkeys who lived in the hills surrounding their monasteries and temples came down and smoked from the long wooden opium tubes out of natural monkey curiosity, and soon found themselves hooked. The monks took advantage of this situation by training the monkeys to pick for them the best tea leaves from high and inaccessible places before they were allowed the narcotic fix.

Whatever the facts of this unlikely story, there is evidence from ancient writings that the Chinese believed that the best quality tea leaves came from the least accessible places, and so trained monkeys to be lowered in baskets to pluck leaves from sheer mountainsides. What is certain is that some tea in Ming times was considered so rare that it was only for the emperor. One of these teas, contemporary writers say, was harvested by tormenting monkeys on steep slopes so that they would tear branches off tea shrubs and hurl them down in anger; the leaves would be stripped from the branches, cured, and sent along to the Imperial Court.

Tea does grow best on hillsides, and some of it can be difficult to harvest. There is no doubt that the rarest, most difficult to obtain teas were sent to the court in tribute. It would seem natural that with this attention being given to tea, elaborate ceremonies concerning its drinking would grow up in China. And to an extent such a ceremonial approach did exist.

Transporting bales of tea by river sampan.

The *Ch'a Ching* and other ancient writings emphasise the importance of ritual in tea drinking: water must be boiled in various exacting stages and poured over the tea only when it reaches a state evocatively described as "billowing waves." Lu Yu outlines nine steps that tea must always undergo in its manufacture, and seven in the brewing. He talks of 24 implements that must be used each time, and says the ritual is so important that it is better to forget your cup of tea altogether if even one of the implements is missing. He even goes so far as to lay down guidelines for what the conversation while drinking tea should consist of, showing contempt for "would-be connoisseurs" who can do no better than note smoothness and shades, adding that "Others will tell you it is good because it is yellow, wrinkled and has depressions and mounds. They are better judges. But the really superior taster will judge tea in all its characteristics and comment upon both the good and bad."

Leisured gentlemen would always have in their houses special rooms for the preparation of tea and special rooms for its consumption, and something approaching a Tea Ceremony enjoyed brief vogues in both T'ang and Sung times. But the Chinese for the most part, and very early, dropped elaborate ritual trappings; there was no real, continuing development of a true Tea Ceremony. This was left to China's neighbours, the Japanese, who incidentally were among the most avid readers of the *Ch'a Ching*.

By Lu Yu's time, China had become the greatest empire in the world and was trading, via caravans, as far West as Persia, and by ship, east to Japan, where in the 8th century the blind Chinese priest Ganjin arrived with Chinese medicines and brick tea. Although China was by now a refined tea drinking nation, the first and still the only tea-drinking nation, some of its inhabitants were still so crude as to chew chunks from the bricks while they drank hot water. The Japanese, on the other hand,

Grace and dignity at the Japanese Tea Ceremony (Sha-no-yu).

were quick to adopt the ultra-refined process of grinding the tea to a powder to be mixed with water.

By the early part of the 9th century, the true and lasting success of tea, leading to the Tea Ceremony, or *Cha-no-yu*, meaning "the way of tea," was being established in Japan. One of the best descriptions of the ceremony, as it was developed over the succeeding centuries and is conducted still in modern-day Japan, comes from the Irish-Greek journalist-historian, Lafcadio Hearn, one of the few foreigners ever to receive Japanese citizenship. The Tea Ceremony, Hearn wrote in the 19th century, "requires years of training and practice to graduate in the art... Yet the whole of this art, as to detail, signifies no more than the making and serving of a cup of tea. However, it is a real art — a most exquisite art. The actual making of the infusion is a matter of no consequence in itself: the supremely important matter is that the act be performed in the most perfect, most polite, most graceful, most charming manner possible. Everything done — from the kindling of the charcoal fire to the presentation of the tea — must be done according to rules of supreme etiquette: Rules requiring natural grace as well as great patience to fully master."

The teahouse in Japan is considered so important that a special architecture, known as *chaseki*, was developed for it. The basis of the conception is the simplicity of a forest hut, decorated with some calligraphy, a painting or a flower arrangement. On the outside are teahouse gardens, known as *roji*, which contain carefully placed stone water basins and lanterns. The guests are greeted by the host in these gardens, and led to an inner *roji* where they pause to rinse their hands and mouths at one of the stone basins. Each element of the garden is named and has an exact purpose, such as the stone outside the middle gate where the host meets his most important guest.

The ancient Chinese had some elaborate teahouses too, often with impressive forecourts, sometimes part of palace complexes. But more commonly the Chinese teahouses have been relatively modest, and certainly far less exacting, in conception. There was sometimes strict etiquette observed in a Chinese teahouse: The host presented the cup of tea with both hands as a gift while speaking pleasant words. And the Chinese went to great lengths to see that the proper atmosphere was maintained. Only servants who were even-tempered were allowed in the special rooms where tea was made and where tea was drunk. Even so, most teahouses in ancient China, like those existing today, were meeting places for friends and merchants, places to relax and pass the time pleasantly, perhaps doing a little business or perhaps showing off treasured caged birds. Starting in the Sung Dynasty, *dim sum*, special titbits, mainly in the form of delicate dumplings, accompanied the tea. And often musicians provided entertainment playing traditional works on traditional instruments. Although sometimes Chinese teahouses have matched their Japanese counterparts in tasteful

decoration, there has never been the tension found in so many aspects of life in Japan.

In general, it is safe to say that the Chinese have always displayed a greater catholicity in their tastes than their exacting Japanese cousins. The tea that is always used in Japanese ceremonies is powdered green tea, and everywhere you go in Japan the tea that is served you, in whatever form, is invariably light, unfermented green tea. Although in Lu Yu's time fermented black teas seem to have been generally favoured, we know that by the Ming Dynasty, the time when the Chinese adopted steeping as the favoured method for brewing, they were also experimenting with varieties of tea much as we know them today — the greens, the well-fermented blacks, some of which are similar to Ceylon teas, and also the semi-fermented tea that we know now as oolong.

Under the Manchus, tea was not only relished, it was glorified as much as it had ever been: History records a Ch'ing Emperor, Ch'ien Lung, as the author of the oft-quoted line, "You can taste and feel, but not

describe, the exquisite state of repose produced by tea, the precious drink which drives away the five causes of sorrow."

After the fall of the Manchus and establishment of the Republic, a period of great decadence set in that was to last until the communist triumph in 1949. This decline had, among other things, a profound effect on tea drinking habits. Teahouses, as many old Asia hands fondly recall, became something more than places to gossip, drink tea and relax. Now you could, between cups, lie in a special room on an opium divan, or in an equally special room with one of the sing-song girls who had become the primary teahouse entertainers.

Such intriguing factors aside, the search that began before the time of Lu Yu for ever-better tea has never ended. The communists are now applying modern market research techniques in order to come up with more popular pure teas and blends. The Westerners who intruded upon China in Ch'ing times were as taken with the tea as they were with the rich silks and other luxury goods and the more carnal delights they found. As early as the 17th century tea imported from China was enjoying a great vogue in parts of the West, and in the declining years of Manchu rule the British planted tea in India and Ceylon and became major producers in their own right.

Still, the "nice hot cuppa," hastily brewed and adulterated with milk by the English when under stress; the stagnant, dark concoction out of samovars that is an essential element for any figure in a Russian novel who is going around the bend; the tea bag, whose shape is promoted with more gusto than its contents and the instant (sometimes right down to lemon and sugar) powders with which the American media assaults Americans night and day; plus such other corruptions as the mint tea of North Africa and the billy tea of Australia — all must seem extremely strange to the refined gentleman of Chinese descent — who *knows* that tea will always be China's drink.

How the West (and

Thomas Twining 1675-1741

When Sir Edmund Hillary and the Sherpa guide, Tensing, conquered the summit of Mount Everest in 1953, they took tea with them to the top of the world. And it may well have helped them triumph in the last savage stages of the climb. As Hillary remarked later in what must rank among history's greatest testimonials to any beverage: "During our ascent of Mt Everest, tea constantly gave us cheer and vigour."

When Lieut-Col John Glenn climbed even higher in February 1962, riding *Friendship* 7 through the heavens to achieve a record-breaking three orbits of the earth, one of the first things he asked for when he landed was iced tea.

In 1973 two Finnish psychologists wrote a comically plaintive letter to the long-established London tea merchants, Twinings, describing themselves as "two tea-connoisseurs, possibly the two most mentally disturbed," and pleading for more tea. "We are the Finnish tea champions (we think)," they wrote. "One evening we had at least 25 cups of tea each. That evening one of us lost his senses in a great euphoric attack. The intoxication for the other one was more gradual. In spite of this the tea was very refreshing. Unfortunately we got so refreshed that we later in the evening forgot to count."

A year later Samuel Twining, the ninth generation director of the famous family business, launched himself on a promotional tour of Hong Kong, Japan, Australia, New Zealand and Iran — six of the no less than 90 countries to which Twinings teas are exported. In Hong Kong he found that local agents were expecting their sales to double in the ensuing twelve months. In Australia, sales of the company's speciality teas had doubled for two consecutive years, and on a per capita basis the Australians were now recognised as being among the world's greatest tea drinkers consuming 4 lbs per head a year.

But Sam Twining had a few words of caution to offer on the things they do with tea in Australia, particularly brewing it in aluminium tea pots and using woollen tea cosies. "The best tea pots are made of earthenware, crockery, stainless steel or silver — aluminium turns the tea blue," he warned. "Tea cosies, those awful woollen things old women like to knit, certainly keep the pot warm, but as well they keep the extraction process going — and you end up with stewed tea."

In 1975, statistics showed that the world tea consumption had risen 25 percent in a single decade, and tiny New Zealand, with its population of only two million people, had suddenly emerged as a dark horse challenger to the absolute world supremacists of the "hot cuppa," Britain. New Zealanders were now consuming 5½ lbs of tea per head a year, the survey showed, but Britain was still firmly entrenched at the top of the tea-drinking table: though their consumption had dropped slightly over the previous 15 years, Britons were still sipping and guzzling about 8½ lbs of tea per head per year — a performance that inspired one Fleet Street writer to heady eloquence:

"Tea is much more than a mere drink in Britain. It is solace, a mystique, an art, a way of life, almost a religion," wrote Cecil Porter of *Gemini News Service*. "It is more deeply traditional than the roast beef of old England (now priced out of the market for many of us). It is at least as characteristic of Britain as Yorkshire pudding, bowler hats, rolled umbrellas, the Guards, and fish and chips. This khaki-coloured concoction brewed, through an accident of history, from an exotic plant grown thousands of miles from fog, cricket and left-hand driving, has become the life-blood of the nation."

Indeed, this "concoction" was fast becoming the life-blood of much of the developed world. In 1977, statistics released by the Tea Board of India and the International Tea Committee had some surprising facts and trends to show on the true extent of the world's tea production and consumption.

India, the world's greatest tea-exporting nation for the past 150 years, was now holding back 60 percent of its annual production for an expanding domestic consumption. The United States, reacting to sharp rises in coffee prices, had boosted its imports of Indian teas by 70 percent in one year and was now recognised as the world's second biggest tea buyer — a status that finally put to death the pro-coffee, anti-tea myth that has hung around since the historic Boston Tea Party two centuries ago.

Apart from China, Taiwan, Vietnam and the Arabian and Persian Gulf states, the review listed no less than 40 nations which qualify as major or noted tea consumers — each having a total apparent consumption of more than two million pounds a year. Britain and the Soviet Union were the two giants of the tea league, with the British consuming a total 400 million lbs of tea a year and the Russians knocking back 234 million lbs

annually. The Republic of Ireland was showing an amazing capacity for the cuppa; while its annual average consumption totalled only 23 million lbs, its apparent consumption per head of population ranked close to Britain's — around seven-and-a-half pounds a year. Other leading tea-drinkers, in descending order of annual consumption, were the United States and Canada, Pakistan, Turkey, Australia, Iran, Iraq, South Africa, Sudan, Morocco, Egypt, East Germany, France, Hong Kong and Denmark.

But while the consumption figures pointed to a growing worldwide taste for tea, production statistics gave an illuminating picture of the extent to which the tea bush itself had spread across the globe. Kenya, for example, which is nowadays viewed as a future African challenger to the traditional tea centres of Asia, had increased its tea exports to Britain from three-and-a-half

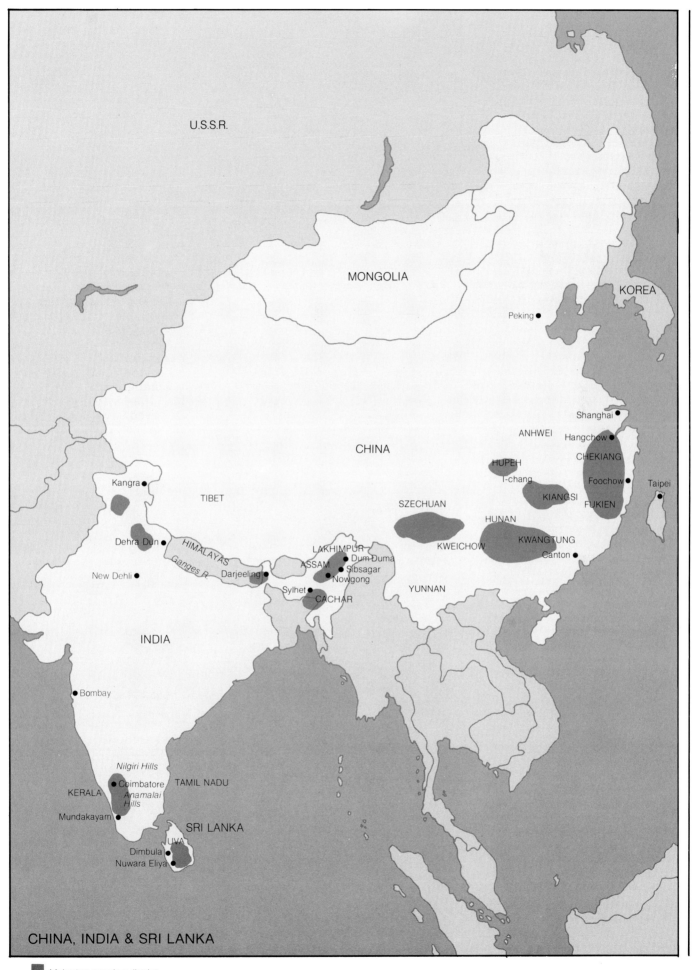

U.S.S.R.

MONGOLIA

KOREA

Peking

Shanghai

ANHWEI

Hangchow

CHINA

CHEKIANG

HUPEH

I-chang

Foochow

Taipei

KIANGSI

Kangra

SZECHUAN

FUKIEN

TIBET

HUNAN

Dehra Dun

HIMALAYAS

KWANGTUNG

KWEICHOW

LAKHIMPUR

Dum Duma

Canton

Ganges R.

Darjeeling

ASSAM

Sibsagar

New Dehli

Sylhet

Nowgong

CACHAR

YUNNAN

INDIA

Bombay

Nilgiri Hills

TAMIL NADU

KERALA

Coimbatore

*Anamalai
Hills*

Mundakayam

SRI LANKA

UVA

Dimbula

Nuwara Eliya

CHINA, INDIA & SRI LANKA

Major tea growing district.

million pounds in 1951 to a whopping 56½ million lbs in 1976. And while China, India and Sri Lanka had long been identified by the average tea drinker as the sole fountainheads of the tea industry, a most incredible list of tea-producing countries now emerged — Indonesia, Bangladesh, Kenya, Uganda, Tanzania, Malawi, Mozambique, Mauritius, Rwanda, Argentina, Brazil, Japan, Taiwan, Turkey, South Vietnam, Papua New Guinea, Peru and Equador.

Plainly, tea had all but won the West, and with the price of its main rival, coffee, climbing to around five times its own cost, the rest of the world lay open to it. For over 4,000 years, tea had been a closely guarded secret and social refinement of fabled Cathay — the Middle Kingdom. Now, in the relative flicker of history, in just three centuries, it had burst forth like the flavour of its own brewed leaf to seduce and indeed revolutionize the social tastes and habits of five continents. And, incongruous as it may seem, the paths that it took and the adventures that it inspired along the way provide the composition and colours of a broad and epic canvas of history.

Tea's first great ocean-spanning leap took it to Japan, a society which in ancient times bowed and aspired to the grandeur of China's T'ang dynasty, with its wealth and many marvels, in much the same way in which we tend to look to New York or Los Angeles today. As early as 729 AD, the Japanese emperor presented powdered China tea to 100 priests who attended a four-day reading of Buddhist scriptures in the palace at Nara, and many of the clerics planted the new shrubs when they returned to their own districts. The historic meeting resulted in the first record of tea cultivation in Japan. "Gyoki, 658-749 AD, spent his life building forty-nine temples, each with its garden of tea plants. For over a century after (the emperor's) inspired gesture, enthusiastic Japanese monks and emperors worked hand in hand spreading tea throughout Japan."[1]

When, in later years, the emperor's capital was moved

JAPAN

■ Major tea growing district.

Tea producing areas of Japan (top) and terraced tea gardens in Ceylon (above)

Shade and irrigation balance a fluctuating climate in a southern China tea plantation.

The tea industry of Java — legacy of the colonial Dutch.

from Nara to Kyoto, the new imperial palace included a Chinese-style tea garden, and a new government post of Supervisor of Tea Gardens was created. But tea had not yet become a social drink, and the Supervisor of Tea Gardens was not exactly the forerunner of today's commercial plantation managers. "Since the position was part of the government's medical bureau, it is apparent that the early Japanese tea drinkers respected the beverage, as did the first Chinese users, for its curative powers."[2] This early flowering was shortlived, however, as tea gardens and the infant tea culture were trampled under almost two centuries of political upheaval and brutal civil war.

Meantime, tea began trickling out of China toward the West. Around the 7th and 8th centuries, shortly after its special qualities and social pre-eminence had been celebrated, almost deified, by the scholar Lu Yu in his renowned *Classic of Tea*, it spread gradually and naturally along the overland trade routes radiating from the borders of what was then the Celestial Kingdom, the greatest empire on earth. Caravans from Persia carried it away in tubs and casks alongside "exotic cloth sewn of golden thread and feathers and woven gauzes as delicate as smoke."[3] The plant took root, in fact, along the ancient caravan paths that snaked through the misty northern mountain ranges of Assam, Burma and Siam — a phenomenon that has since triggered fierce debates on whether China, or indeed Assam, was the region in which tea truly originated.

MALAYSIA

Pematangsiantar ●

SUMATRA

HALMAHERA

(BORNEO) KALIMANTAN

SULAWESI (CELEBES)

WEST NEW GUINEA

Jakarta ●

Pengalengan Plateau

JAVA

INDONESIA

■ Major tea growing district.

While merchants and hilltribes fostered the spread of tea toward the West, priests kept it alive in strife-torn Japan and, when the bloody fighting finally ended there, sponsored a tea "renaissance" that was to elevate the plant and its bitter-sweet beverage to a lofty social and spiritual level of Japanese society. Tea was first introduced to Japan as a sort of accompanying stimulant to a new school of religion — Zen Buddhism, based on the Chinese Ch'an school founded by the Bodhidharma (the Japanese call him Daruma). Zen evolved as a reaction against the trappings of organised Buddhism, just as Protestantism was to sweep away the pomp and ceremony of Holy Roman Christianity much later in Europe. The Way of Zen refined Buddhism down to "the simple clarity of intense meditation ... to experience the Infinite within."[4] And a popularly quoted story recounts how, as early as the 6th century — shortly before the Japanese emperor first handed out the powdered tea to those 100 priests — the monks brought Zen teachings back to Japan along with tea, which they carried to help them stay awake during the long sessions of meditation.

However, something of a controversy surrounds exactly who it was to first introduce Zen to Japan, and when. According to the Schapiras, in their definitive account *The Book of Coffee and Tea*, Zen reached Japan in 1191, at the close of the civil wars, when the monk Eisai returned from China. "Eisai was not only the first to introduce Zen Buddhism into Japan; he also started a tea renaissance. He brought new seeds from China which he planted near the castle of Fukuoaka on Seburi Mountain and in the temple grounds of Shokokuji. He also wrote the first Japanese work on tea, *Kitcha-Yojoki* or *The Book of Tea Sanitation*, in which he describes tea as a divine elixir of the gods." Controversy aside, one thing is certain: Zen and tea flourished side by side throughout the island empire, each complementing the other. Zen, with the intense and almost bizarre questions and answers of its *mondo* sessions — "What is the sound of one hand clapping?" — provided a simple discipline, without the need for books, which appealed to the rigid disciplines of Japan's military-dominated, class-structured society. Tea, with its caffeine-based capacity for stimulating the body and expanding the senses, became an integral part of the Zen ceremony, with its search for *satori*, the Infinite Oneness. Gradually, tea itself transcended medicine and the esoteric cloisters of religion and, as its appeal broadened among the laity, became the centre of a ritual regarded as the epitome of social refinements, the Tea Ceremony. And the simple, brooding aestheticism of the Tea Ceremony has underscored the tone and style of art, philosophy and social etiquette in Japan from that moment on.

But while, by the year 1300 AD, tea had become a popular beverage and social ritual throughout Japan and China, it would be almost two more centuries before it captured the attention of the West and then yet another 200 years before it began to grace the Western table. Chinese junks were trading and marauding throughout Asia, and by the 15th century they were sailing as far west as the Persian Gulf and Arab ports and Somaliland. Marco Polo had made his historic voyage to China in the 13th century, returning to the West in a fleet of four-masted junks. As already mentioned, Persian caravans had been plodding back and forth over the Asian mainland since the 8th century — and, indeed, China tea had already become a popular drink in the courts of the conquering Tamerlane. But Persia was still *Asia*, and as far as the lusty, warring feudal states of Europe and the British Isles were concerned, tea was little more than a strange, slightly bitter drink that peculiar pig-tailed people with barbaric customs insisted on poisoning themselves with in distant lands that were closer to myth than reality in the average imagination. By all accounts, the spread of tea virtually stopped dead for something like 400 years. As one of the most noted contemporary writers on tea, Sir Percival Griffiths, commented: "In view of the considerable

Above and opposite page: Chinese tea plantations — now aiming for a new dominance.

29

intercourse between China and the West during the first millennium after the discovery of tea, it is strange that no knowledge of either the plant or the beverage reached Europe before the sixteenth century."[5]

Even then, the first official record of tea in the West was simply a reference in a book written in 1559 by Giambattista Ramusio, secretary to the Council of Ten in Venice, which was then the central clearing house for trade between East and West. Ramusio wrote what a Persian merchant named Hajji Mahommed had told him about the herb *Chai Catai* which the people of Szechuan were accustomed to infuse in boiling water to help relieve stomach aches and gout. Explorers, missionaries and merchants subsequently brought back more reports of this peculiarly bitter medicinal drink, but for many years it was still presented as a palliative rather than a beverage.

"Understandably, the accounts (were) confused," Denys Forrest writes in his social and economic history, *Tea for the British*. "Some told how the leaves were barbarously boiled

up in an iron kettle; others had the more delicate notion that (as in the Tea Ceremony to this day) they were first pulverized, and that the infusion took place in the bowl from which it was subsequently drunk. It may be convenient here to summarise the then current impressions about oriental tea-making in the words of a somewhat later observer, John Nieuhoff, who visited Peking with a Dutch East India Company embassage in 1655:

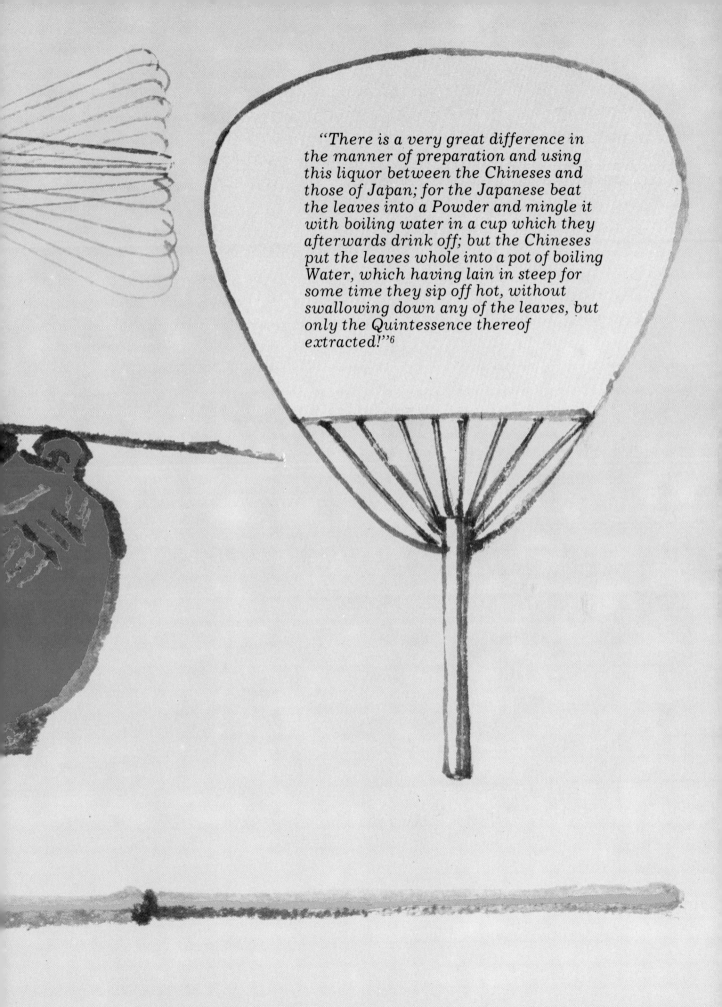

"*There is a very great difference in the manner of preparation and using this liquor between the Chineses and those of Japan; for the Japanese beat the leaves into a Powder and mingle it with boiling water in a cup which they afterwards drink off; but the Chineses put the leaves whole into a pot of boiling Water, which having lain in steep for some time they sip off hot, without swallowing down any of the leaves, but only the Quintessence thereof extracted!*"[6]

From the time of the first mention of tea in the West in 1559, another half a century was to pass before Westerners actually set eyes upon any substantial amount of it. And it may come as something of a surprise to dedicated tea drinkers that the world's greatest tea-drinking nation, Britain, dragged its feet behind the other European nations, neither importing tea first nor first attempting to cultivate it, nor even engaging in the first real trading of tea as a commodity. During this 16th century, a great era of Western adventurism and discovery, the Elizabethan buccaneers of England, the Dutch and the Portuguese rounded the African Cape and burst across the Indian Ocean to probe the Malay Peninsula, Japan and the China coast, each competing for trade in spices and the fabled riches of the East. The Portuguese got there first, and as early as 1557 they established a trading centre on the island of Macau at the mouth of China's Pearl River estuary. Later, they became the first Westerners to set foot in Japan, and their Jesuit priests eventually became powerful commercial and political advisers to the Japanese rulers. The Portuguese were the first to write home about tea — yet for many years they did little more than talk about it.

In 1560, Father Gasper da Cruz, the first Portuguese Jesuit to preach Catholicism in China, returned home to describe the "bitter, red and medicinal" beverage that he had encountered in China. Another Jesuit, Italian Father Matteo Ricci, who became scientific adviser to the Chinese court, maintained that it promoted Chinese longevity and vigour. Another longstanding student of Chinese customs and social refinements, Father Alvaro Samedo, described how the serving of tea to a guest was an honour to him, but the third cup was the sign for him to get up and leave.[7]

While the Portuguese talked about it, the Dutch became the first explorer-traders to actually take it back to the West. Supplanting Portugal's trading position in the East, they first shipped China tea to their trading centre in Bantam, Java; then, in 1610, the first Chinese and Japanese teas were carried, along with huge cargoes of oriental luxuries — silks, spices, porcelain — from Bantam to The Hague. There, the aristocrats and wealthy merchant classes took up tea-drinking as a showy and rather daring novelty. "Before tea was shipped in enough volume to sell at a reasonable price, outlandish tea gatherings were held that resembled bizarre parodies of the Japanese tea ceremony. Tea that cost the equivalent of $100 per pound was served from silver and porcelain containers with much pomp and ceremony. Sugar and saffron were added to the beverage, which was sipped noisily from a saucer. Conversation was monopolised by the tea, and rich cakes served with it. When as many as fifty cups had been drunk by each guest, brandy, sugar, raisins and pipes — smoked by the women as well as the men — ended the party."[8]

By this time the Dutch had also become the first Western cultivators of tea, opening up tea plantations in Java. By 1640 they were shipping tea home in such large amounts that tea-drinking spread through the lower levels of Dutch society, and what had first been the centre of exclusive, fashionable orgies for the extremely rich now became a more dignified drawing-room enjoyment for middle-class and more common people. Says Denys Forrest: "By the mid-1650s quite a brisk trade was being done in Holland, though the tea was mainly sold in ounce packets by apothecaries; later it spread to the 'colonial warehouses' which were the predecessors of the modern grocer's shop."[9] By 1650 the Dutch had also begun spreading tea around the rest of the Western world. Peter Stuyvesant took it to North America, to the newly-settled Dutch trading post called New Amsterdam, later to be renamed New York by the conquering British. And in 1657 the first public sale of tea in Britain itself took place — and it was Dutch tea.

Jan Verkolje painting of Dutch drinking tea from imported Chinese porcelain.

What had the British been up to while this exciting new tea cult had been burgeoning around them? Not much, according to the historians. Though, as early as 1615, the first authenticated reference to tea by a Briton had been made in a letter by the East India Company's agent in Hirado, Japan — requesting shipment from Macau of "a pot of the best sort of chaw" — so far as the importation and widespread drinking of the beverage was concerned, even the French had beaten them to it. Denys Forrest observes that tea, introduced into France by the Dutch, became the height of fashion there while it was still hardly known in Britain. "By 1648, a Paris physician was referring to it as 'the impertinent novelty of the age'; Cardinal Mazarin took it for his gout; Racine (French dramatist, 1639-99) was an addict and so was Paul Scarron, husband of Madame de Maintenon (later to become the mistress and then secret wife of Louis XIV), while later in the century we owe to the greatest of letter-writers, Mme. de Sevigne, some of the earliest recorded instances of the use of milk with tea in Europe."[10] Strangely, this burst of passion for tea reigned in the *salons* of Paris for only a few decades, and within 50 years of its introduction the French palate had returned to its traditional tastes, coffee and chocolate. Why this tremendous reverse happened, no-one is entirely sure, though the Schapiras comment that at the height of its fashion tea "set off the kind of raging debate the French are celebrated for, including wildly varying opinions from medical, religious and governmental circles,"[11] and James Laver, in his delightfully witty introduction to the history of Twinings, suggests that tea — a much milder drug than coffee — just didn't lend itself to the inherent French passions.

"A learned German has written a treatise in which he strives to prove that national drinks and national characteristics go together," Laver writes. "Certainly the notion is not nonsense. The coffee-drinking France of the eighteenth century produced the *Encyclopedistes* . If they had tried to conduct their logical arguments on a foundation of wine, they would either have cut one another's throats in the first two hours or fallen asleep in the third or fourth. For the end of wine is sleep, but the end of coffee is wakefulness. Tea, I cannot help thinking, is less logical. It neither promotes sleep nor stimulates argument. Rather does it induce a sense of genial well-being, which may well be the foundation for our English 'genius for compromise'."[12]

Just as the British were the last of the three great Western European adventurers to break into the China and East Indies trade, so were they the last to begin savouring the "lusty leaf" of brewed tea. But, just as their belated arrival in the East heralded an aggressive battle for trading supremacy, culminating in an empire, so did their introduction to tea spark off a growing clamour for it that resulted in possibly the strangest social phenomenon of contemporary history — an entire nation addicted to the drink. If James Laver's concept of a tea-based "genius for compromise" is correct, it can certainly be said that the British hardly displayed the same moderation in getting their hands on the stuff.

The true date of tea's first arrival in Britain is not easy to pin down. It depends on whether ounces or pounds, or hundreds of pounds, are regarded as volume enough to constitute an official "arrival." But a fairly clear chronology of several debuts can be pieced together, beginning somewhere between 1652 and 1654 when, according to one source, "the first tea to reach England arrived with a British admiral who had discovered a small amount in the galley of a ship he had captured from the Dutch."[13] The first official imports reached London in 1657, when Dutch tea was put up for auction at Garway's Coffee House. Coffee had been introduced into Britain from the Middle East some 20 years before, and, with coffee houses proliferating around inner

London, it had made considerable inroad into the traditional British beverage, ale. Now, Garway's were introducing a liquor which, if the outrageous claims of their advertising could be taken seriously — and it was! — would put ale, coffee and indeed most other libations and palliatives to death:

"Those very nations famous for Antiquity, Knowledge and Wisdom do freely sell it among themselves for twice its weight in silver," the auction posters blared; and they went on to list tea's many medical virtues covering such things as "Headache, Stone, Gravel, Dropsy, Scurvy, Sleepiness, Loss

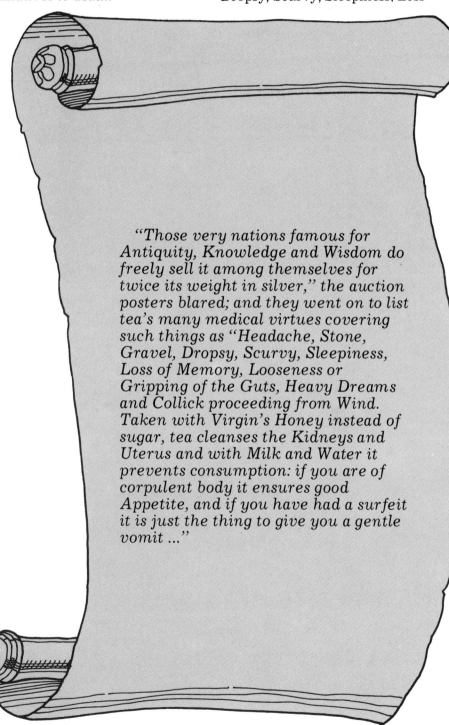

"Those very nations famous for Antiquity, Knowledge and Wisdom do freely sell it among themselves for twice its weight in silver," the auction posters blared; and they went on to list tea's many medical virtues covering such things as "Headache, Stone, Gravel, Dropsy, Scurvy, Sleepiness, Loss of Memory, Looseness or Gripping of the Guts, Heavy Dreams and Collick proceeding from Wind. Taken with Virgin's Honey instead of sugar, tea cleanses the Kidneys and Uterus and with Milk and Water it prevents consumption: if you are of corpulent body it ensures good Appetite, and if you have had a surfeit it is just the thing to give you a gentle vomit ..."

of Memory, Looseness or Gripping of the Guts, Heavy Dreams and Collick proceeding from Wind. Taken with Virgin's Honey instead of sugar, tea cleanses the Kidneys and Uterus and with Milk and Water it prevents consumption: if you are of corpulent body it ensures good Appetite, and if you have had a surfeit it is just the thing to give you a gentle vomit ..."[14] Tea was certainly a novelty. And two years later it was still so new that the diarist Samuel Pepys wrote: "I did send for a cup of tea (a Chinese drink) of which I had not drank before."

As with the Dutch a half-century before, it was the aristocracy of Britain, beginning with the monarchy, that gave tea its first stamp of social approval. In 1662, after the British had challenged and broken the Portuguese dominance of trade with China from Macau, King Charles II married the Infanta Catharine of Braganza in a royal union that was obviously aimed at thrusting a double-edged blade at the Dutch in the East Indies. Part of Catharine's dowry was a Portuguese gift to the British of the island of Bombay, which eventually became the Far East trading headquarters of the British East India Company.

Catharine is otherwise noted for bestowing upon the British — or upon the court and nobles, at least — the "beneficient habit of drinking tea."[15] Two years later the British finally entered the China trade, the East India Company opening up a trading "factory" in Macau, and the merchant-mariners sent a "handsome gift of tea and cinnamon oil in a silver case" to Charles and Catharine. In 1668, the Company began shipping tea back to England as a commodity for the first time — carrying 134 lbs of best Dutch tea from Bantam, Java. Of this, 21 lbs were given to the Queen, and the custom of drinking tea at court began in earnest. A year later the Company shipped another 143 lbs and the novelty of tea drinking became a social occasion, with much etiquette, and a meal. "It was the host or hostess who brewed it, and from the 1670s comes the introduction of fine cups, bowls, saucers, pots, ladles, spoons, trays, caddies etc., made of silver, pewter and pottery."[16]

As society embraced it, tea began to pour into England in regular and increasing amounts. And as it filtered down through the various levels of society, it underwent, at the hands of the confused and inexperienced,

brewing and drinking practices that would have made the venerable "father" of the Chinese tea ceremonies, Lu Yu, roll painfully in his grave. To the British and many Europeans, tea was "mysterious, dear and quite puzzling. Some took tea with salt, ginger and nutmeg. A Jesuit who had enjoyed tea in China added eggs to his tea. Schoolboys spread used leaves on their bread. A country housewife, thrilled with her first pound of the fashionable stuff, invited neighbours to share it. She boiled it and served it rather like spinach with salt and butter. Her guests detested it."[17] Nevertheless, the infant tea cult persevered. Early records show that from 1668 to 1689 the East India Company shipped regular cargoes of tea home from Bantam, where they had bought it from Chinese traders, and from Surat, north of Bombay, where it came from Portuguese merchants trading out of Macau. In 1684 the British finally reached their cherished goal in the Far East; having established their own trading post, or "factory" as it was called, in Macau, they began dealing directly with the Chinese. Five years later the Company's ship *Princess* sailed from Amoy to London carrying the first tea

imported directly from China to England. A fierce, tumultuous and bloody trading era had begun — an age in which commerce, empirical conquest and national honour became hopelessly confused. And at home, the first impulses were already stirring in what was to become a national craving for tea.

Among the most noted early promoters of tea were the seventh Duke of Bedford and his Duchess, Anna. In the 1790s, the duke imported 10 lbs of tea "as well as utensils for drinking tea,"[18] and may well have been the first to launch a new term into the household vocabulary in England — "china" tea sets. His wife, on the other hand, is accredited with pioneering the essential ritual that ultimately doomed Britain to wholesale addiction — the ritual of "taking tea."

Up until that time, according to the contemporary tea chroniclers, Charles and Violet Schafer, mealtimes in England were a lusty, almost barbaric affair of red meat and ale. "Country houses in their day provided prodigious breakfasts with joints of beef on the sideboard. Sportsmen drank ale,

scorning such 'slops as tea.' And they went hungry until dinnertime about 8.00 pm. Lunch as a meal did not exist. Anna (Duchess of Bedford), to put a stop to this punishing routine, introduced tea at 5.00 in her rooms. This humane custom originated at Belvoir Castle where the duchess often visited. Although tea was expensive, she happily shared the luxury with other ladies staying at the castle and served it with cakes. She continued the practice when she returned to town and sent cards to friends promising 'tea and a walk in the fields.' By degrees, afternoon teas became the fashion."[19]

Tea was to transform social habits. It wasn't long before it was establishing a completely new class of retail business throughout Britain. By the 18th century "tea grocers, as distinguished from those who did not carry the leaves, began selling tea to wealthier London families, and the new drink started making its first appearance in Scotland and Ireland."[20] By then, imports were spiralling year by year. Whereas in 1699 some 40,000 lbs of tea were entering Britain each year, by 1708-17 the annual imports had burgeoned six-fold to 240,000 lbs. Tea imports were monopolised by the East India Company, and through its trading alone "the spread of tea was enormous, covering the British Possessions and across the Atlantic to North America."[21] As in France, the new beverage quickly touched off something of a national wrangle in England. Naturally enough there were gentry who disdainfully dismissed tea-drinking as "a base Indian practice," and one prominent doctor wrote that tea was the source of "hypochondriac disorders." But even then, the English passion for the brew heavily outweighed the wowsers, and in 1744 it gained ecclesiastical support. George Berkeley, the Irish Bishop of Cloyne and an idealist philosopher, virtually declared it suitable for Christian consumption. "Tea water," he said, "is of a nature so mild and benign as to cheer but not inebriate." And around this time,

the immortal Samuel Johnson admitted that the benign habit had got him well and truly hooked — describing himself as a "hardened and shameless tea drinker who for twenty years diluted his meals with only the infusion of the fascinating plant; whose kettle has scarcely time to cool; who with tea amused the evening, with tea solaced the midnight and with tea welcomed the morning."[22]

By 1750, less than a century after the first official shipments arrived from Java, Britain's tea imports had reached what was then the relatively staggering amount of 10 million lbs a year — and had conclusively acclaimed tea as the new national drink.

Britain wasn't the only nation to succumb so completely to tea. The Russians, too, were seduced by the beverage — their capitulation taking little more than 50 years from the moment, in 1618, when the Chinese embassy in Moscow presented several chests of tea as a gift to Czar Alexis. In 1689, when Russia and China signed the Treaty of Nerchinsk to establish a common border, regular camel-caravans began transporting hundreds of pounds of tea via Mongolia. The caravans followed one of the longest, and most tortuous, overland trade routes the world has ever known: "The entire trip from China to Russia was 11,000 miles and took 16 months. Tea was shipped from the producing regions to the northern part of Tientsin. Horses and mules struggled to bring the tea 200 miles over the mountains to Kalgan, northwest of Peking. Then the tea travelled by camel 800 nightmare miles across the Gobi desert to Kyakhta, and from there to Russia. After the Trans-Siberian Railway was completed in 1905, tea took only seven weeks to reach Russia, and the mighty caravans faded into history. Genteel Russian ladies could no longer say with pride that they were sipping 'caravan tea'."[23]

John H. Blake gives a more definitive account of the Russian camel-trains in *The Tea Gardens of the World*, published some two years before the Trans-Siberian Railway revolutionized the Sino-

Russian tea trade. Writing at a time when "China's present tea-trade with the White Czar's Empire is, in round figures, equal to 117 million lbs annually," Blake observes: "This includes the very finest leaf produced, as well as the coarser varieties made into bricks which are intended for the consumption of Siberians, the poorer classes of Russians and Russian Asiatics. The best teas required for consumption in Russia — for the Russian is very particular about the quality of his tea — are manufactured and packed with exceeding care, and are now sent by steamer to the Black Sea port of Odessa, while the coarser varieties, after having been powdered and compressed into tablet and brick form ... are despatched overland by means of camel caravans. Brick-tea, although sent by caravan, is not what is known as 'Russian Caravan Tea,' for the latter is an extremely high-grade, specially prepared black tea which the Russians carry overland by camel caravan in order to prevent the deterioration consequent upon a long ocean voyage."[24]

All this was happening, of course, around 1903 — two centuries after tea imports into Russia began in earnest. It was in the beginning of the 18th century, in fact, that the Russians embraced tea on a widespread scale. The camel caravans were stepped up, the volume of trade increased, and this brought tea prices down to a level where rich and poor alike could enjoy the brew. Tea soon became widely accepted as a hearty, warming and sustaining beverage ideally suited to the Russian way of life. The steaming samovar, a bubbling combination hot water heater and teapot which could serve up to 40 glasses of tea at one time, became one of the popular symbols of Russian society — hot, sweet tea ready at any time to warm the body and soul after a day in the often sub-zero temperatures. And, like the five o'clock teas in Britain, it changed the Russian eating habits. "The Russians drank a mixture of one-quarter tea and three-quarters hot water with lemon or jam, sipping it from glasses through a sugar cube held between the teeth. Since by tradition and for economic reasons the Russians were accustomed to eating only one large meal a day, the giant samovar was a pleasant and inexpensive way of seeing them through the rest of the day."[25]

But Russia succumbed to tea with relative peace and a certain grace compared with the public clamour, political furore and widespread under-the-counter practices in support of the brew that were going on in Britain. On one hand, tea had inspired a vast public outburst of eloquence infused with sentiments that approached absolute ecstacy. Consider the tribute paid by Colley Cibber, Poet Laureate in 1750: "Tea, thou sober, sage and venerable liquid, thou female tongue running, smile soothing, heart opening, wink tippling cordial to whose glorious insipidity I own the happiest moments of my life, let me fall prostrate." Or the prayer of thanks uttered a century later by one Sydney Smith: "I am glad I was not born before Tea." Comments poured, in fact, from all sections of British society, ranging from the more jaundiced view of one observer in 1742 that "the meanest families, even the labouring people in Scotland, made their morning meal of tea to the disuse of ale," to the plea of an Eton College student, William Dutton, in a letter to his father in 1766: "I wish you would be so kind as to let me have tea and sugar here to drink in the afternoon, without which there is no such thing as keeping company with the other boys of my standing."

By the end of the 18th century, tea had become "a very sedate, conservative element in the country's life, especially at the domestic level" — immortalised by the tragic poet William Cowper as "cups that cheer but not inebriate," hailed as an important social flux between the sexes, "taming the rude strength of the one and ennobling the graceful weakness of the other" — (Denys Forrest suggests that "Allow me, Madam, to fill the teapot for you" was a

recognised social, or even amorous gambit) — and it had even been taken up by the nation's temperance reformers as a front-line weapon against alcohol. "The idea that the words 'tea' and 'teetotal' are connected is usually dismissed as a piece of folk etymology. But I am not so sure," Forrest writes. "The (temperance) tea meetings of the period had a double function, to recruit abstainers and to raise money. It is pleasant to read how the thing was done in Preston at Christmas in 1833. Over 1,000 tickets were sold in advance, and finally 1,200 people sat down by relays at tables 630 feet long, while in Mr Halliburton's yard a 200 gallon boiler was chuffing away. The big moment came when a band of 40 reformed drunkards, with TEMPERANCE printed on their aprons, entered as waiters. In fact, reports of similar events suggest that the presence of 'great numbers of reformed characters, respectably clad' was one of the attractions always laid on."[26]

But tea had triumphed against a vivid backdrop of medical opposition, parody and even vilification. In the eyes of some reactionaries, tea, or rather the afternoon tea rituals, had become associated with loose gossip and scandal. As the tea cult cut into the government's revenue from a malt tax on ale, one Member of Parliament protested that "Tea drugs and debases working-class women!" Doctors branded it as a "pernicious drug." In 1748, John Wesley, founder of the Methodist Church, came out fiercely against tea, claiming that it had given him "symptoms of a Paralytick disorder." Wesley wrote that he had subsequently discovered many other people in London who were similarly afflicated by tea — "nerves all unstrung, bodily strength quite decayed" — and he led hardened tea addicts of his London Society in a sort of mass "cold turkey" as the first step toward renouncing the brew. "For himself, the test was hard. During three days his head ached and he was continually half-asleep. By Wednesday afternoon his memory had failed completely

and he sought a remedy in prayer. The next day all his symptoms had vanished. He was a cured man."[27]

William Cobbett, the Radical politician and journalist, launched the sort of attack on tea that still echoes today through the boardroom level of British society — condemning the valuable working hours lost through the national preoccupation with the "slops of the tea tackle." If only an hour was spent each day on the tea-drinking ritual, he complained, that added up to a total waste of 30 working days a year. As for tea's effect on the health, he saw it as a poison. "Put it to the test with a lean hog. Give him 15 bushels of malt and he will repay you with tenscore of bacon. But give him 730 tea messes, and nothing else, and at the end of about seven days he is dead with hunger." Another noted pamphleteer, Jonas Hanway, placed tea in the same barrel as gin, which contained such unsavoury ingredients as oil of turpentine and sulphuric acid, in a polemic entitled *AN ESSAY ON TEA. Considered as Pernicious to Health, obstructing Industry and impoverishing the Nation* .... The charge was answered by none other than Samuel Johnson, that "hardened and shameless tea-drinker," but even Johnson admitted that tea was, because of its lack of nourishment, "a Liquor not proper to the lower classes of the people" — and then he pointed directly at a far more pernicious and proven social problem that the tea cult had given Britain. "If tea is thus pernicious, if it impoverishes our country, if it' raises temptation and gives opportunity to illicit commerce, which I have always looked on as one of the strongest evidences of the inefficacy of our government and the corruption of our people, let us at once resolve to prohibit it for ever."

The "illicit commerce" that Johnson referred to was nothing less than the wholesale smuggling of tea into Britain — a national racket so widespread, and so freely condoned by all classes of tea drinkers, that in 1777 a vicar, the Reverend

Tea, green and serene on a plantation.

Woodforde, wrote how he had purchased "at 10/6d a pound of tea from Andrews the smuggler."

Tea, like almost every other popular, wide-selling social commodity in contemporary Britain, had come to the revenue-raising attention of H.M. Customs & Excise. As early as 1660, the king had been granted excise duties on tea, in its brewed, liquid state, sold at the 2,000 or so coffee houses that had proliferated throughout London. In 1689, the system was replaced by a duty levied on dry leaf released for home consumption from the bonded warehouses of the sole importers of tea, the East India Company. As imports grew, so too did the levies. "From that day until, after countless adjustments, the last of the duties was abolished in 1964," Denys Forrest writes, "politicians never ceased to fiddle with the taxation of tea." In 1695, an extra shilling was added to the tea duty to pay for

the movement of troops to fight the Battle of the Boyne in Ireland in 1690. By 1773, the tax represented about 64 percent on the auction value of all teas, and tea became a contraband commodity as highly-prized as the proverbial "brandy for the parson" around Britain's wild southern coasts. It's estimated that between 1763 and 1769 ships of France, Holland, Portugal, Denmark and Sweden — competing with the East India Company monopoly — were carrying between 10 million and 13 million lbs of tea a year to Europe, half of which was "earmarked for eventual smuggling into the United Kingdom!"[28] The anti-tea pamphleteer Jonas Hanway wrote how fleets of smugglers' cutters ferried tea to Devon and Cornwall from the Isle of Man, where they paid the island's proprietor, the Earl of Derby, a private "duty" of a penny per pound on their illicit cargoes. Scotland later became the main landfall for tea smuggled in from Scandinavia. "There was hardly a man, woman, child or conniving innkeeper in the surrounding countryside who would not help conceal tea in caves, deep cellars and church crypts once it was ashore. Highwaymen on horseback posted tea to clandestine buyers anywhere in the country. Pack horses and strings of pony carts galloped through the night loaded with tea. Duffers padded themselves with as much as 100 lbs of tea on a single carry. For a price, local shepherds drove their flocks over telltale tracks left on sandy beaches by passing gangs. So many carters were at work smuggling that a shortage of farm labour existed in some districts."[29]

The rising excise duties had also spawned another, far more nefarious figure in the illicit tea industry — the adulterator. "British tea," a mixture of inferior or soiled imports, had appeared on the market around 1710. By 1725, laws were being passed with fixed penalties for "dealers, manufacturers or dyers" who adulterated the "true China leaf" with sloe-leaves, liquorice-leaves and the leaves of tea which had been used before by mixing and staining them with *terra japonica*, sugar, molasses, clay, logwood etc.[30] And tea drinkers were no doubt horrified to read, in 1784, a description by Richard Twining, third generation head of the pioneer tea merchants, of a particularly odious — not to say poisonous — method of "making *smouch* with ash tree leaves to mix with black teas.

"When gathered they are first dried in the sun and then baked. They are next put on the floor and trod upon until the leaves are small, then lifted and steeped in cooperas, *with sheep's dung*, after which, being dried on a floor, they are fit for use."

With bootlegging and counterfeiting reaching such unhealthy proportions, it was obvious that either tea would have to be banned, as Samuel Johnson had suggested, or the excise duties lifted. Getting rid of tea was by now out of the question: Too many people were willing to go to almost any length to enjoy it. More than half the tea being sold in Britain had come in by way of the smuggler's cutter. So, in a move recognised as one of the great milestones of the development of the tea industry, the tax was drastically slashed by the Commutation Act of 1784 and the smugglers put out of business — but not before one of the most epochal dramas of the story of tea had been played out, a drama which was to have a profound impact on the course of modern history: the Boston Tea Party.

Since its introduction into the North American colonies by the Dutch around 1650, tea had become as socially fashionable as it was in Britain and other parts of the Old World. Welcomed first in New Amsterdam, it really established itself as a social cult when the British wrested the settlement away from the Dutch in 1674 and renamed it New York. "Tea gardens were built around the town in emulation of the London pleasure gardens (Vauxhall and Ranelagh). Tea, coffee and hot rolls were served at all hours. Entertainment consisted of fireworks, band concerts, dancing and evening strolls down walks lit by lanterns."[31] Street vendors wandered about offering "tea water" from the choicest wells and pumps. The tea cult soon spread into the New England settlements, where the colonists were initially as confused about the technique of tea drinking as their brethren back in Europe. In Salem, now synonymous with another cult, witchcraft, the first tea drinkers boiled their leaves for hours, producing a harshly bitter drink, then sprinkled the mash with salt and butter and ate it.

A scene after the British government's reduction of the tea tax (1785).

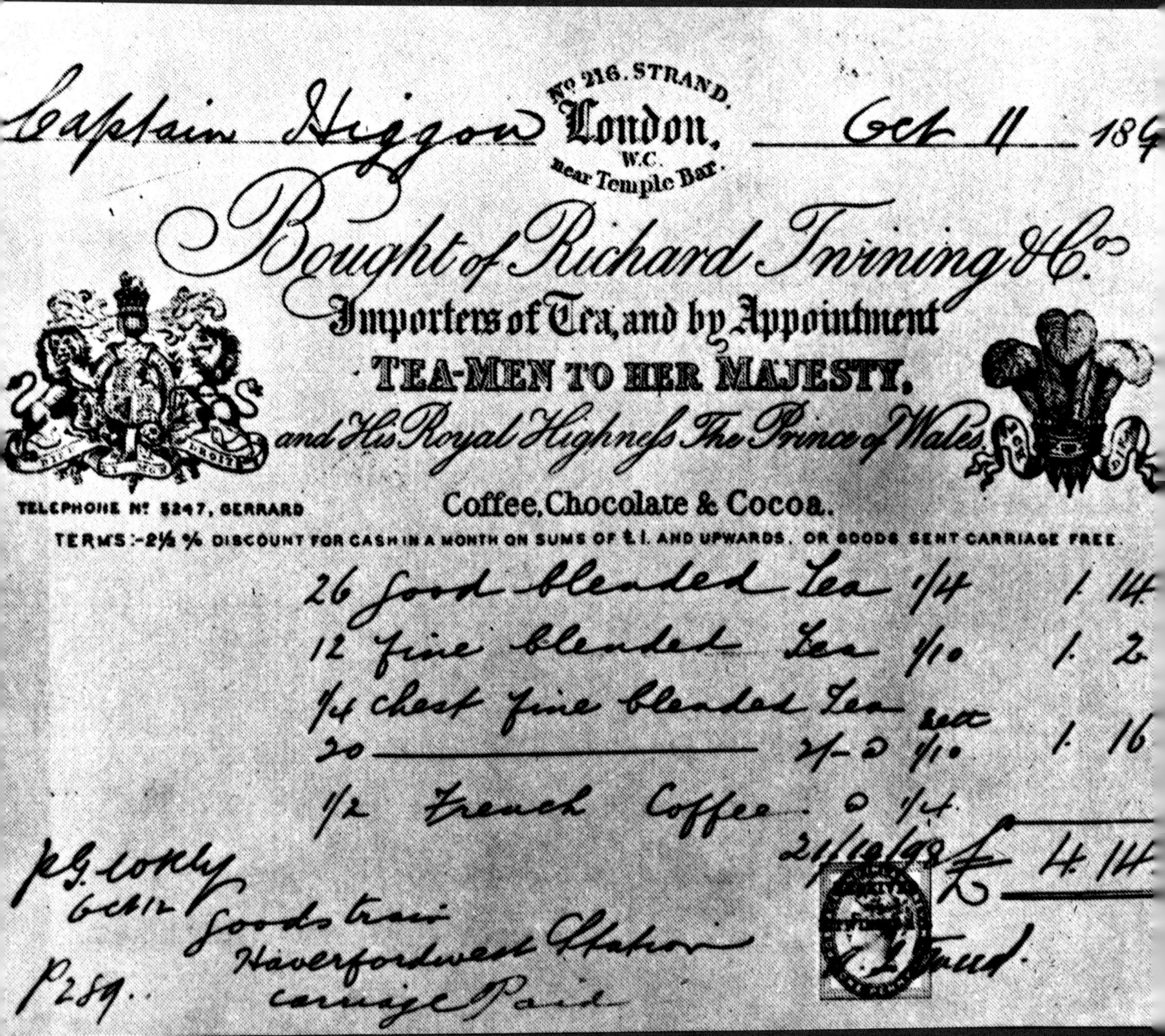

Captain Higgon

No 216. STRAND,
London,
W.C.
near Temple Bar.

Oct 11 189_

Bought of Richard Twining & Co

Importers of Tea, and by Appointment

TEA-MEN TO HER MAJESTY,

and His Royal Highness The Prince of Wales

Coffee, Chocolate & Cocoa.

TELEPHONE Nº 5247, GERRARD

TERMS:—2½ % DISCOUNT FOR CASH IN A MONTH ON SUMS OF £1. AND UPWARDS. OR GOODS SENT CARRIAGE FREE.

26	Good blended Tea	1/4	1. 14
12	fine blended Tea	1/10	1. 2
¼ chest fine blended Tea			
20	——— 24-0 1/10		1. 16
½	French Coffee 0 1/4		
	21/10/99	£	4. 14

pd. cash
Oct 12   Goods train
              Haverfordwest Station
P 289.   Carriage Paid

By 1760 the colonies were importing a total one million lbs of tea a year — three-quarters of it smuggled across the Atlantic by the Dutch. Social etiquette was centred around the tea-table. "Beautiful silver, porcelain and earthenware pots, cups and saucers along with richly-grained wooden tea trays and tables had evolved around the new beverage."[31] George Washington was one of the New World's noted tea addicts, taking tea with toast or cakes at breakfast and supper. (So attuned was he to tea, in fact, that he became one of the very few post-revolutionary American figures to continue drinking what by then was a very unsocial beverage).In 1796, Thomas Twining, a son of Richard Twining, visited "The General" in Philadelphia. Washington was by then three years away from retirement as the first President of the United States. After a 45-minute conversation that ranged over such subjects as India and the discovery of coal in America, "the General invited me to drink tea with him that evening," Twining recounted. "I regret to say that I declined this honour on account of some other engagement — a wrong and injudicious decision, for which I have since reproached myself."

By and large, tea had by that time disappeared from the American table. Its demise had marked the rise of the War of Independence and the birth of the nation that George Washington now led. Tea had been betrayed by taxation, and taxation had virtually robbed the British of what would have proved to be their mightiest commonwealth. Looking back from the 20th century, it is plain that the Westminster politicians who "never ceased to fiddle with the taxation of tea" manipulated, in this instance, possibly the greatest political blunder of British history.

As in Britain, the price of tea imported and sold in North America carried a hefty excise loading — hence the vast amounts being smuggled in by the Dutch. In 1767, this tax was rolled back, bringing the price of

English tea in New England down by eightpence a pound. Meanwhile, however, the Stamp Act of 1764 had been passed, asserting the right of the British Parliament to impose internal taxation on the colonists, resulting in angry protests and a boycott of British goods. In 1766, the Stamp Act was repealed, but parliament retained the right to tax the colonies and this sparked off another round of demonstrations in Boston. A year later the Treasurer, Charles Townshend, compounded the dispute by putting taxes on "a number of imports into America, of which by far the most conspicuous was tea."[32] This aroused a fresh wave of colonial anger, and another trade boycott in which the colonists began seeking their own substitutes for imported goods. "Tories kept on drinking tea when they could smuggle it in as snuff or tobacco. Other colonists substituted 'Liberty Teas.' These they brewed from four-leaved loosestrife (a herbaceous plant), Labrador tea (manufactured from a root with a 'very physical taste'), balm, ribwort, sage and leaves of currant and raspberry. Patriots, students, children and women took the pledge. A poetess publicly bade farewell to her teacups, saucers, cream jug, sugar tongs and pretty tea chest."[33] In 1773, Parliament

passed the notorious Tea Act, which was aimed at allowing the East India Company to make good on thousands of pounds owed to the government by exporting and selling surplus tea stocks in America — complete with a "mulishly required threepence a pound tax."[34] For militant protesters in Boston and other New England ports, this was the last straw. On December 16, 1773, with three East India Company ships, the *Dartmouth, Eleanor* and *Beaver*, moored with their tea cargoes in Boston Harbour, a group of about 50 colonists organised by Samuel Adams staged "the most impudent example of colonial protest," yet one whose consequences were as historic as the shot, three years later, that "rang around the world."

"As darkness fell, cryptic messages were whispered about *mingling tea with salt water*, and a band of men moved off towards Griffin's Wharf. Imaginative engravings show them elaborately disguised as Redskins, but in fact most of them made do with a dab of paint or lampblack, and an old blanket around the shoulders. In turn they boarded the *Dartmouth*, the *Eleanor* and the *Beaver*, and for the next three hours nothing was heard but 'the steady whack-whack of hatchets' as the chests were split open and the contents

The patronage of high society at the turn of this century is reflected in Twinings' many Royal Warrants.

tipped into the sea. According to one participant, the water was only two feet deep at this point, and the tea piled up on the surface, forming great windrows along the beach next morning."[35] A total 342 chests of tea valued at £10,000 went into Boston Harbour. There were other less dramatic protests in Charleston, where tea was left on the wharves to rot, and in New York, where whole consignments were sent back to England — but the Boston Tea Party provided the battle-standard and the rallying cry of the colonists in a bitter deadlock that led ultimately to the War of Independence and the American Revolution. One of the revolutionary leaders, John Adams — who was to become the second President of the United States after Washington — put into majestic words the role that he considered tea played in the birth of America.

"The people should never rise, without doing something to be remembered — something notable and striking. This destruction of the Tea is so bold, so daring, so firm, intrepid and inflexible, and it must have so important Consequences, that I can't but consider it as an Epocha in History."

For the British, this "destruction of the Tea" resulted in costs that went even further than the humiliation of losing the American colonies; for, with cruel irony, they were forced to foot the bill for the ill-fated war against the rebel colonists and their French and German allies by paying even higher duties on their beloved tea. The 64 percent duty that existed at the time of the Boston protest was hiked up to 106 percent by 1782, rose again to 114 percent a year later, and by the time the Commutation Act was passed in 1784 it had reached an all-time high of 119 percent. Naturally, smuggling became even more rife, graduating from "caves, cutlasses and ponies trotting through the dark ... into a highly organised commercial enterprise which threatened the legitimate trade with ruin."[36] Some 250 ships of up to 300 tons and armed with as many as 24 cannon were now regularly running tea into Britain from Dutch and French ports. Once ashore, this contraband tea — up to seven million lbs a year — was retailed through smugglers' syndicates that operated so cheekily that they even carried insurance with Lloyds.

Faced with such an alarming national racket on the one hand, and the adulteration of tea on the other, the government finally moved to stamp out both iniquities by dramatically slashing the tea tax from its ceiling of 119 percent to a mere 12½ percent. The Commutation Act was the work of the Tory Prime Minister William Pitt, and it has gone on record as one of the very few positive achievements of his two terms of office, in which he led Britain into a costly war with France, triggered an the Irish rebellion and was out-manoeuvred by Napoleon. Certainly, the act put large-scale smuggling out of business. Though the tax was raised again to around 100 percent after 1806 to help pay for Britain's role in the Napoleonic Wars, the smugglers never again regained the power to dominate and virtually dictate Britain's tea industry. (In 1818, however, there was still a booklet at large in London published by the "London Genuine Tea Company" giving hints on the detection of adulterated teas).

Though the smugglers had, in fact, played a vital role in the spread of tea — keeping the British market supplied at a time when taxation threatened to drive tea-drinking out of fashion — the industry gained a much healthier footing when they were finally out of the way. In the twelve months after the Commutation Act was passed, the sales of duty-paid tea leapt dramatically from five million to 13-million lbs. A year later, in 1786, the doyen of the British tea merchants, Twinings, was able to report, with obvious relish: "The average quantity of tea sold by the Company for ten years prior to the passing of the Commutation Act was little more than six million of pounds weight per annum; but within the first twelve months after the act took place, the quantity sold exceeded 16 million pounds." By the year 1800, Britain's entire consumption of tea had doubled within a period of 50 years, and now stood at 20 million lbs; and the industry entered that grand era of trade and empire in which British sovereignty was almost everywhere to be seen. As Sir Arthur Bryant observes in *The Age of Elegance, 1812-1822*: "Everything testified to (Britain's) wealth, power and empire: the interminable masts in the Thames, Tyne and Mersey, the Chinese, Persian, Parsee and Armenian traders in the Customs Houses, the Souchong Tea that Dorothy Wordsworth wrote from Rydal to Twinings" — (she had ordered 75 lb of Souchong and 30 lb of Congou "to be sent by canal.")

For tea, it was an exciting and tumultuous era, beginning with the second great milestone in its history of expansion in Britain — the removal of the East India Company's import monopoly. Throughout the greater part of the 18th century, rival City of London merchants had been struggling to break the company's trading monopoly on tea and other luxuries from the Far East, first commissioning and operating their own trading fleets under Dutch and French flags, then engaging in the wholesale smuggling that grew out of the atrocious excise duties on tea. In turn, the East India Company was a victim of sorts of a Chinese trading monopoly in Canton, called the Co-Hong, which regarded Britain's trading supremacy with infuriating disdain — Chinese edicts and proclamations against the British merchants usually ended with the command: "Tremble fearfully hereat. Instantly obey!" — and forced the Company to buy tea at a higher price than that offered to free-traders from Holland, Portugal and the infant United States. In 1813, the East India Company's power was arrested for the first time in 250 years when trade with India was thrown open to all British merchant houses with appropriate trading licences — but the Company managed to hang on to its China monopoly. It wasn't until 1834 that this "odious monopoly," as one rival

Indiamen at Whampoa.

East Indiamen load China teas at Whampoa.

described it, was broken, and within weeks of the historic abolition dozens of merchant houses, brokers and retailers were opening up in Britain's main ports and trading fleets were beating out of Liverpool, Glasgow and Bristol to join the tea trade in Canton. The East India Company "Select Committee" gave way to a swashbuckling brand of free-traders, or "merchant princes," who fought tooth and nail for supremacy in the China trade and who soon began clamouring for a safe and sovereign trading haven off the coast of China and well out of the reach of the detested Co-Hong. In 1841 the Union Jack was raised at a place called Possession Point on the sandy northern shore of an island that Lord Palmerston was to derisively label "a barren rock with hardly a house upon it." The free-traders, the Jardines, the Mathesons, the Dents, called it Hong Kong.

All this took place against a black backdrop in British trade which, in present retrospect, can only be described as a blatant and dishonourable drug war. By the time the East India Company's monopoly was abolished, the tea trade was already so enormous that the Chinese quite justifiably believed that the English couldn't live without it. At the same time, it was a trade that constantly threatened Britain with a crippling deficit. For one thing, the Middle Kingdom imperiously dismissed just about everything that Britain offered in return for tea — the Emperor Ch'ien-lung informed King George III at the height of the Ch'ing dynasty: "I set no value on strange or ingenious objects and have no use for your country's manufactures ...." For many years there was only one commodity that the Chinese would accept, silver bullion; and as the domestic demand for tea grew, Britain's treasury reserves dwindled alarmingly. Something else was needed for exchange, and in the 17th century, after the East India Company established itself in India, the British came up with it — opium, grown in Bengal and exported through Calcutta. By the time the

The tea clipper *Cutty Sark*.

The clipper ships *Taeping* and *Ariel*

48

Company lost its Charter in 1834, opium was being shipped into China at the rate of 16,000 chests a year. In the following five years the trade increased to nearly 40,000 chests. The terms of trade were now reversed: "Silver that had flowed into China to pay for tea and silk now flowed out to pay for the imported opium."[37] In a bid to stop this financial drain and the debilitating effect that opium was having on its society, the Chinese court banned the drug — a move which led to smuggling, increased trading and military pressure from the British culminating in the so-called Opium Wars, and the gradual disintegration of China's sovereignty at the hands of the major European powers. And amid all this strife, there was that one shameful chapter in the history of tea, a period when two nations — the Chinese with their "chah" and the British with their opium — were virtually feeding each other's addictions.

And the British were well and truly besotted with tea by the time the East India Company faded from the scene. Already consuming an average of about two lbs per head a year, their national craving was such that the free traders leapt into the Far East commerce with one prime aim in mind — to bring tea to England faster than their competitors. But hardly had their private "tea navies" of lumbering, fat-bellied, cannon-bristling East Indiamen begun hauling their tea cargoes into London and Liverpool than the Americans burst into the business with a new type of ship that rendered the British vessels obsolete — the Yankee Clipper.

The world will probably never again see sailing ships, or a sailing era, to rival the great tea Clippers of the 1850s and 1860s. Just as the Clippers represented the absolute, triumphal match of speed and sail, so did they mark the beginning of the end of sail as a means of transport. But before their relatively short heyday was over, they established a romance and a series of maritime records that have never since been surpassed nor even repeated.

Modified from swift privateers built in Baltimore for the War of

1812, the Clippers embodied design and performance concepts that were virtually tailor-made for the post-1834 tea trade, in which premium prices went to the first teas to reach Britain's docks and skippers were awarded big cash bonuses for beating the rest of the field home. With speed more essential than tonnage and safety, their hulls — built of timber planking on iron frames — were streamlined pencil-thin compared with the East Indiamen, and their three masts carried 2,000 or more square yards of sail. Their tea cargoes were literally crammed into the hulls — the chests even "beaten into place with huge wooden mallets until the outer ones formed themselves to the lines of the ship"[38] — so that they wouldn't shift as the vessels crashed, heeled and plunged through the seas under full sail. These ships were a magnificent blend of beauty and utility — tightly-packed floating tea chests with enormous crowns of sail; and they were, and still are, the fastest sailing vessels man has ever known. One of the first American-designed Clippers, the *Flying Cloud*, raced from Foochow to San Francisco around Cape Horn in 89½ days. Another, the *Lightning*, set an all-time speed record of 18 miles an hour on a 24-hour burst in which she covered no less than 436 nautical miles. The *Rainbow* covered the voyage home to New York so fast that she was the first to bring news of her own arrival in Canton.

The first Yankee Clipper to arrive in London, the *Oriental*, was able to get twice the going price for her 1,600 tons of tea than her British competitors. Not only that, but her owners demanded, and were paid, a freight fee for the run that represented two-thirds the cost of the ship's construction. After the British merchants had recovered from their shock, they quickly abandoned their old East Indiamen and began laying keels for their own China clippers. By 1853 they had caught up with the Americans; the British-designed *Cairngorm* matched the American vessels in speed and later embarked upon a series of exciting duels with the fastest of the American rivals, *Sea Witch*, whose speed records still stand on the books today. And so began the celebrated, unforgettable, near-legendary Great Tea Races of the 1860s.

"Each year tea clippers raced home to collect the premium for the first cargo to sell at auction in (London's) Mincing Lane. Captains and crews were the best. Public interest was so high citizens placed bets. Winner of this marine derby was the one who first hurled sample boxes of tea ashore to waiting clerks who drew samples and rushed them to Mincing Lane. Handsome cash rewards went to victorious captains and crews."[39]

The greatest tea race of all took place in 1866. It was also to be the last, for already "on the horizon a reek of smudge heralded the arrival of the steamship, or *smellpots* as they were known. May 28, 1866, dawned as usual along the South China coast, hot and humid. The cook fires from Foochow, just up the Min River from the Pagoda Anchorage, could be smelt by the sailors in the roads. There was an air of expectancy as the men waited for the opening of this year's tea market. Massed at anchorage

were the finest ships in the China tea trade: *Thermopylae, Ariel, Black Adder, Taeping, Serica*. A majestic sight, the cross hatch of tall masts and yard arms against the rising sun, tars aloft in the rigging, mates screaming pidgin down into the graceful Chinese lighters, decks swarming with coolies racing to load before the ebb-tide. Finally they were loaded, sheets to the wind, sailing hard down the China coast. Nine ships left the Pagoda Anchorage that day on the same tide, all hands racing home to England with prize money in their eyes.

"Not a single extra man was carried and all men were able-bodied seamen. This was no pleasure cruise. Through Typhoon Alley they raced and on into the Indian Ocean, rounding the Cape of Good Hope with acres of canvas aloft. On the morning of September 6th, the anxious shipowners had a surprise. Rounding the headland at the mouth of the Thames, pennants up for a pilot, the *Ariel* shot into view. A cry went up. Ten minutes later there was another cry as *Taeping* hove into sight, followed several hours later by *Serica*, all on the same tide from halfway around the world."[40]

For three short but glorious decades the Clippers were the aristocratic masters of maritime commerce. They packed the East Indiamen off into history and left even the then ultra-modern steamships floundering in their wake. The steamers couldn't compete because their cargo-carrying capacity was severely reduced by the amount of coal they had to take aboard for the long voyages around the tip of Africa. But when, three years after the Great Tea Race, the Suez Canal was opened and the steamers became a more economic proposition, the magnificent Clippers in turn fell into obsolescence — the last of their proud breed, including the immortal Cutty Sark, serving out their days in the relatively mundane business of carrying wool from Australia.

The *demise* of the East India Company and the great tea Clippers coincided with an even more momentous decline, followed by a remarkable rebirth, in the history of the tea industry. In short, China lost its historic tea-growing monopoly, and, for the British market at least, India and Ceylon became the new masters of the tea trade.

Tea had been taking root on a relatively small scale outside China and Japan from the moment the Western adventurers first hove-to off the strange, unknown coasts of the Far East. The Dutch had begun cultivating tea in Batavia (now Jakarta) as early as 1684, and after a series of political twists and turns and false starts their plantations were flourishing throughout Java and Sumatra by the 1870s. The British knew that tea was indigenous to India as early as the mid-1600s, but were so obsessed about breaking into the China trade that they literally gazed upon the horizon and ignored the ground at their feet. And when, in 1788, Sir Joseph Banks recommended that tea be cultivated on a large scale in India, the East India Company, fearful of losing the monopoly that it had on the China teas, managed to get the proposal pigeon-holed. Even when Major Robert Bruce discovered wild tea plants

Fiery Cross

Thermopylae shortening sail before a storm.

growing in the hills of Assam in 1823, the Company was able to block plans for large-scale cultivation. By 1830 there had been experimental tea plantings in Penang, St Helena, Brazil and even the United States territory of Carolina; and in Britain, free-traders and merchant princes opposed to the East India Company monopoly were questioning why their tea-drinking nation should be forced to *kow-tow* to the cantankerous Chinese when tea could apparently be grown on a subcontinent which, by then, was virtually sovereign British soil.

The fall of the East India Company quickly resolved that *impasse*. Within five months of the abolition of the monopoly, the Governor-General in Calcutta, Lord William Bentinck, set up a tea industry committee that despatched George James Gordon to China with orders to bring back plants and seeds. Gordon found that his mission wasn't as easy as read: The Chinese mandarins had no intention of allowing foreign devils to get their hands on the secrets, or even the seeds, of their most prized industry.

However, Gordon did manage to get some seeds, which were grown in Assam and South India, but later it became apparent that Chinese plants and methods of cultivation were just not suited to the Indian soil and climate.

Another sortie into China was made in 1843 by the Scottish botanist, Robert Fortune. Obviously aware of Gordon's problems, Fortune resorted to a bit of subterfuge which would have done justice to the plot of any "Carruthers of MI5" thriller. He "talked his way into the forbidden interior of China disguised as a Chinese in order to collect plants and seeds from tea plantations. In the process, he uncovered the Chinese secret that green tea was not from a plant different from that which produced black tea. It was the process that made the difference."[41] Fifteen years later, Fortune went into China again, this time to collect seeds for southern planters in the United States. These were cultivated in the Carolinas, Georgia, Florida, Louisiana and Tennessee, but attempts to establish a large-scale commercial industry failed.

The first Indian tea to be shipped to Britain came, in fact, from the wild bushes growing along the hills of Assam. It arrived in London in 1838 in a series of 38-lb boxes soldered into a tin chest that were in turn encased in wood to avoid contamination on the long sea voyage. A jury of tea experts tested it and declared it "burnt" and rather harsh but nevertheless competitive with the China brands. Another 171 chests were shipped to London and auctioned in 1841 and, in deference to an industry and a tea-drinking public still vastly committed to their traditional China grades, the Assam teas were offered as hysons, gunpowders, Congous and Souchongs. It wasn't until the 1860s that the Pekoes and Orange Pekoes and other distinctive Indian tea designations were advertised openly on the wholesale market. But by that time, Indian teas had become firmly entrenched, with plantations spreading to Chittagong and Sylhet in what is now Bangladesh, to Darjeeling in the Himalayan foothills, to Dehra Dun and the Kangra Valley in the north-west and south to Travancore and the Nilgiris; and the total production had passed its first important milestone of one million lbs a year.

Pioneers of the Indian tea industry were individual British adventurers and families who hacked their way into the hilly jungles, established plantations and, after all the hard labouring had been done, were followed by limited liability companies. The Indian Tea Board's description of the opening up of the High Range in Kerala gives a graphic picture of the hazards that the first tea planters encountered. "The first among them was J.D. Munro who, in 1877, bought from the Pooniat Raja of Anchanaad (a tributary of the Maharaja of Travancore) the main portion of what is now the High Range. These pioneers first began to tame the virgin lands and forests to the needs of man. They tried many crops — coffee, cinchona, sisal, cardamoms — before they found in tea a means to make these reluctant hills productive. The workers faced many dangers — wild elephants, diseases, floods and landslides — before ... their successors were in a position to bring the tools of the best available technology to the developmental task which increased its tempo after 1895, when business houses took over from the individual pioneers. The jungle valleys were increasingly cleared and planted; roads were opened to all parts of the district; the almost insuperable difficulties of transport were met with increasing efficiency first by bullock carts and ropeway (500 bullocks were at one time engaged in the transport of tea), then by a mono-rail system, later by a 2 ft gauge light railway and finally by a combination of ropeways, lorries and tractors."

By 1900, India's tea production had reached 170.5 million lbs, with exports at 164.6 million lbs, of which 154 million lbs went to Britain. An incredible tea revolution had taken place. Whereas in 1859 Britain had been importing 69 million lbs of tea, of which only two million lbs, or three percent, came from India, in 1900, the total British imports stood at 250 million lbs, of which 55 percent came from India and

only five percent from China. And by now, even the fledgling tea industry of Ceylon (Sri Lanka), established in the 1870s when a blight destroyed the island's rich coffee industry, was supplying 37 percent of Britain's imports — seven times the amount shipped in from China.

Why had China's tea industry and its volume of exports crashed so disastrously? For one thing, cultivation had been seriously disrupted by Russian, and then Japanese, moves into Manchuria, by increasingly violent confrontations between the rule of the Empress Dowager and the belligerent trading manoeuvres of the Western powers. At the same time, British teas grown in India and Ceylon were undercutting the more expensive, but finer Chinese teas on the British market; and this forced the Chinese producers to lower the quality of their teas to compete with Indian prices, so that by 1903 John H. Blake was observing that "the deterioration of many of (China's) best known district teas, and adulteration of some, as well as the artificial colouring or 'facing' of others, has been painfully apparent."[42]

British tastes had changed, too. For better or for worse, they were now overwhelmingly attuned to the "strength, thickness and blackness of liquor" of the broad-leafed Indian teas rather than the more subtle flavour of the Chinese leaves. The British had also found that they could get more

cuppas from each pound of Indian tea — three hundred, in fact — and that, according to one British trade official's survey in 1895, just about put the kiss of death on the China blends. "China can never hope to produce a tea which will compare with Indian according to the only standard which now seems to be applicable in England; the standard of strength; the capacity to colour to a certain point of darkness so many gallons of water to each pound of tea."

China had been able to salvage some of the huge trading loss with increased exports to Russia, which in 1903 stood at around 117 million lbs a year. The United States, too, had remained faithful to the Chinese teas, its imports in 1902 touching almost 61 million lbs. (Following Commander Perry's 1854 expedition that broke down the closed doors to Japan, America had also been importing a great deal of Japanese tea — 34½-million lbs in 1902). But China's predominance in the huge British tea market had been smashed, perhaps forever. And amid the national clamour for Indian teas with that proverbial quality of allowing the teaspoon to stand upright in it, only a few voices rose in loud lament of the vulgarity, as they saw it, that had triumphed at the British tea-table. "To every Eastern tea-drinker," Henry Norman complained in his book *The Far East* in 1895, "the tea served at the best houses in England would

be a horror. Nobody who has not travelled in the East and arrived, after a day's tramp through a malarious and steaming jungle, at some poor Chinaman's shanty, and thankfully drunk a dozen cups of the beverage, freely offered, can know how delicious and invigorating even the most modest tea can be."

Today, India is by far the world's biggest tea producer and exporter. Its annual production of around 1,000 million lbs and exports of about 450 million lbs a year give it a commanding 33 percent of total world production, with China and Sri Lanka running second with about 13 percent each. Over half of India's yearly production is now being retained for a steadily-growing domestic market. Sri Lanka, on the other hand, exports almost all its tea and thus records export figures very close to those of India — nearly 400-million lbs a year. China's tea production stands at around 380-million lbs a year, and its annual exports of 120 million lbs reflect a continuing large domestic consumption. After seven decades of civil strife, war, communist takeover and the turmoil of Mao Tse-tung's Cultural Revolution, tea still underscores much of China's social and working life. Tea, and the traditional tea-houses, came under attack, in fact, during the reign of the Maoist Red Guards, with the revolutionaries threatening to wipe out teatime in the Cantonese province, Kwangtung, along with the decadent old customs, old habits, old ideas, old culture of the past. This was one Cantonese custom, however, that defied the anti-revisionists: "They re-examined Chairman Mao's teachings and concluded that teatime was 'wrong in form but right in essence;' that it was all right to restore teatime if they distinguished between the new tea breaks and the old bourgeois pastime."[43]

London is still the main auction centre for all 16 tea-producing countries, with upwards of 90 million lbs of tea passing through for re-export each year. One of the biggest exporters is, of course, Twinings,

A typical Hong Kong tea shop *above* and tea cannisters *(page 56)*.

which in 1981 celebrated its 275th year as the premier tea merchandising house in Britain and indeed the rest of the world. In 1978, Twinings exported 18 different blends of speciality teas to over 90 countries and chalked up earnings in excess of £18 million. The company's principal markets are in all Scandinavian and European countries — with France, interestingly enough, gradually switching again from its beloved coffee to become an important consumer of speciality teas. Twinings now have about 23 percent of the French market — its total tea imports at upwards of 10 million lbs a year — and can thank the ill-health of its turn-of-the-century family proprietor for tempting a large number of French palates back to tea.

"Twinings started its (French) exports quite by accident," says the present head of the family, Samuel Twining. "In 1904

Harvey Twining, who suffered badly from asthma, was told by his doctor that he was to go to either Leeds or Paris where the air would suit him better. Needless to say he chose Paris, and being of a flamboyant nature would spend his summers in the elegant resorts in the south of France. There he would assure the clientele of the delights of Twinings tea. Before long he had built up enough contacts and set up a branch of the firm in Paris, and later the shop in Boulevarde Haussman which is still there today."

Sam Twining sees tea, particularly the speciality brands, expanding into the growing vacuum left by rapidly inflating coffee prices, especially in Europe and the United States. He's also confident that the harsher caffeine content of coffee will ultimately drive more and more people over to its more subtle, light-bodied rival

beverage. "I have a theory that wherever there is heavy coffee drinking there is a greater success in selling speciality tea," he says. "People often suffer from what I call a tortured and twisted palate after too much coffee drinking and do not appreciate ordinary teas and yet enjoy a more definite flavour such as Earl Grey. This has also been proved in Norway, which is a heavy coffee drinking country, where we have a 25 percent share of the tea market. Likewise Finland, where we have a 10 percent share. In Italy, for instance, Earl Grey is very popular" — (in fact, Twinings' exports to Italy rose by 50 percent in 1972 alone, and iced and lemon tea — served mornings and afternoons — have become a fashionable beverage rivalling *espresso* on the boulevarde's of Rome and other major cities).

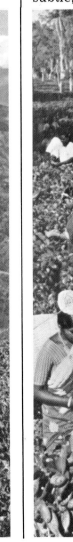

Saris, sashes and mountain scenery on Indian tea plantations.

Britain, and its Anglo-Saxon Commonwealth partners, Canada, Australia, New Zealand, continue to regard tea as less a beverage than an essential of life. Furious debates have raged in London, Vancouver and even New York on the still-controversial matter of whether the brewed tea should be added to the milk, or whether the milk should be poured on the tea; or, indeed, whether milk should be used at all. In Britain, tea is such an integral part of society that in the 1960s Parliament legislated labour laws that included a clause giving British workers the right to two tea-breaks a day. This virtually deified the brew, and led to boardroom concessions that must have made Britain's European neighbours shake their heads in amazement.

"Only in Britain," writes Cecil Porter, "could a county council decide — as Durham did some years ago — to spend $12,000 on two special tea-making rooms. Only in Britain could a group of hospitals (in Derbyshire) appoint an official tea-taster. The importance of tea in British office life was proved in the planning of one of Britain's biggest office blocks with 5,500 workers. At a cost of $880,000 special elevators were put into the building. The lifts carry specially designed urns each delivering 100 non-spill cups of tea."[44]

Through a combination of rising coffee prices, a £3 million promotion campaign by the British Tea Council and vigorous sales drives by Twinings, Jacksons, Brooke Bond, Lyons, Cadbury and other leading tea distributors, Britain's consumption is rising again from the relative slump level of 8½ lbs per head a year that existed five years ago. Speciality teas are being aimed at young couples who switched over to instant coffee when it made inroads into the tea industry after its introduction in 1957; likewise, traditional tea drinkers are being weaned away from their taste for poor quality teas that flooded the market during the severe rationing of World War II. Tea bags, though detested by the connoisseurs, are also driving a wedge into the coffee market, and are expected to command 50 percent of the national tea consumption by the year 1980. Britain's tea imports for domestic consumption and re-export for the twelve months up to mid-1978 totalled an astounding 240,000 tons — that's 487 *billion* lbs — valued at £300 million. With 300 cups to one pound, with all the people in Britain over 10 years of age estimated to drink an average 4½ cups of tea a day, with all workers granted the sovereign right of two tea-breaks a day, is it any wonder that the mystique of tea baffles foreigners. "One Continental critic said: 'Britain could save 247,000 man-hours a week by cutting out tea-breaks'."[45]

Just as it outraged the Hanways and Cobbetts of the 18th century, tea continues to inspire fierce debates among the British pundits of today. On one hand, the British Medical Association has recommended the tea break as a refresher for both body and mind among industrial workers, particularly those in jobs which arouse tension. On the other hand, the feminists are up in arms in support of the people who usually have to make it — the housewives and working women.

"It is the making of tea to pass the time that really starts me screaming," the noted columnist Katharine Whitehorn raged in *The Observer.* "Of all the 182 stupid jobs there are whose only function is to make women who haven't enough to do feel useful, the most tiresome is this useless, boring, time-consuming endless nonsense of tea.

"The news has just hit Britain that tea, the national drink, may actually be bad for you. Some people, it seems, suffer an allergy to it; it makes them twitchy and irritable, gives them strange malaises and unexplained headaches. And all over the country the cry is going up: 'But how can anyone live without their tea?' Darned well, that's how they can live. If you ask me, tea is the national blight and I'm simply delighted if there's any sort of medical case to be made out against it. For if there is one thing that puts more strains on British family life than anything else, it is this appalling prevalence of tea ...."

And so it goes.

A thousand teas

"*Tea is from a grand tree in the south. The tree may grow from one or two feet to as much as twelve. In the rivers and gorges of the Province of Szechwan are trees whose girth is such that it requires two men to embrace them. Those trees must be felled for plucking. Its trunk is suggestive of the gourd and its leaves of the gardenia. The flower is like that of the wild red rose turned white. The seeds are like those of the coir palm. The leaves have the fragrance of cloves while the roots are as those of the walnut.*"

So wrote the poetic pen, or rather calligraphic brush, of the first noted chronicler of tea, Lu Yu, over 1,200 years ago; and while his celebrated *Classic of Tea* laid down Confucian-like rules and etiquette on the growing, preparation and drinking of tea, it was clear that the whole production process was still in its rudest form. The tea of Lu Yu's time was "picked, steamed, pounded, shaped, dried, tied and sealed" into bricks which, powdered and steeped in boiling water, were "whipped to an airy froth." In a fashion to echo the centuries-later birth of the Indian tea industry Lu declared "tea that grows wild is superior. Garden tea takes second place."

It wasn't until the Ming dynasty of the 14th to 17th centuries, an age which saw the Portuguese, Dutch and British first confront the Celestial Kingdom, that the Chinese began steeping the cured tea-leaf in a bowl or cup — and then there began a search for new processing methods and different types of tea. The first Western trading vessels carried two basic teas home with them, black and green. In turn, these were graded according to quality and region of origin. Black teas included flowery pekoe, orange pekoe, pekoe souchong, congou and bohea. Green teas were listed as gunpowder (a greyish, well-flavoured, biting but not bitter tea — certainly not as explosive as it sounds), imperial hyson, singlo, bing and caper.

According to Twinings, whose tea sales records reach back to 1712, "Pekoe — *pak-ho* (white hairs) showed the fine downy tips of the young buds; Souchong

tumult of tastes

A Hundred Years Ago.

Excerpts from "The Observer" of November 22nd, 1835.

Mr. Henry Lytton Bulwer, M.P. for Maryla-Bonne, has been appointed Secretary of Legation at Brussels.

The banking house of Messrs. Twining, in the Strand, which is now approaching completion, is one of the greatest improvements, both in point of architectural appearance and public convenience, which has recently been effected in the vicinity of Temple Bar. Messrs. Twining have been induced to make these alterations upon public grounds, and from a desire to improve the site of their tea warehouse, which has been occupied by members of their family for considerably more than a century.

The turmoil of the election conflict in t'...

— *siau-chung* meaning little plant or sort; Congou — *kong-fu*, i.e., labour (in the preparation of Congou the leaves were handrolled); Bohea — *wu-i*, from the mountains in Fukien, the centre of the black tea country; Hyson — *yu-tsien*, meaning before the rains, or *tu-chun*, i.e., flourishing spring; Singlo or Twankay was the hyson shrub improved by cultivation, it came from Singlo mountain in Kiang Nan. Tea was grown for local consumption all over China,

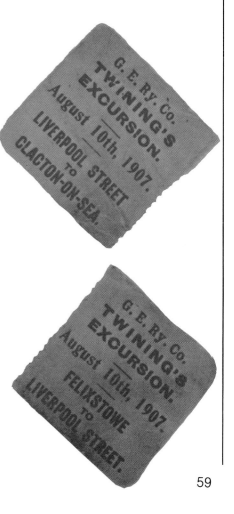

except in the far north, but the provinces that grew the tea for export were in the south-east, Kwangtung (capital Canton), Fukien, Kiangsi, Chekiang, Kiangsu and Ganhwuy. Black and green teas were made from the same plant, the difference being the method of manufacture; green tea was not allowed to ferment and in order to retain its colour, it was faced or glazed with a powdered mixture of gypsum and prussian blue. By far in the way the largest purchases (by the British) were for hyson, then came singlo, congou, bohea, bing, pekoe and souchong, the remaining types only appearing rarely." One of these "remaining types" was an occasional shipment of *oolong*, a tea produced in Fukien province with a smooth, sometimes fruity, often spicy and occasionally smoky flavour brought about by arresting the fermentation process at a certain critical point. Oolong lay in the middle range of the three teas, but whereas the delicate, fragrant green teas became regarded as the "chablis" of the crop, and the rich blacks were acclaimed as the "clarets" and "burgundies," the oolongs, transplanted and refined much later in Formosa (Taiwan), became renowned as the "champagnes" of the tea industry.

Once the British palate, and nervous system, had rejoiced over these three basic categories, the early merchants, distributing through their inner London coffee houses, began adding a new refinement to tea — *blending*, so that around 1715 the ledgers of Twinings' Golden Lyon establishment in Devereux Court near the Temple, were showing bohea mixed with pekoe, congou with pekoe, congou with bohea, bloom green with imperial hyson. The grading itself became something of a science — the various grades aimed not only at superior and lesser tastes but also at hiving off the dregs of the ship's holds to the poorest working man. Bohea was the coarser of the black teas, and singlo was close to the bottom of the list in greens.

"Rock bottom, probably, were Twinings' Green Dust, at between 8s and 12s per lb retail. Black Dust (Bohea) was 12s to 16s and thence you mounted by a steady gradation through some 16 items until you reached 24s to 30s for Congou and 36s for finest Hyson."[1]

Hyson and Gunpowder were the aristocrats, served up in the drawing rooms of England and so jealously valued that many early tea canisters, or caddies, had locks on them to safeguard their contents from servants' prying hands. Bohea, the cheaper "homely" brand was for the liveried and pinafored domestics downstairs. But outside the stately homes, it was the common singlo — rated one grade above the trashy Green Dust — that spread swiftly and widely through British society;

in fact, it can be said that singlo virtually democratized the taste for tea in Britain. As early as 1703 the East India Company's ship *Kent* was given orders that on her return voyage from the East her cargo should include 75,000 lbs of singlo as against 20,000 lbs of bohea and 10,000 lbs of imperial hyson. (Auction prices at this time give an interesting picture of the sort of profits the Company enjoyed with its trade monopoly: The *Kent* was instructed to buy singlo at one shilling a lb; a year later it was put up for auction at 10/- a lb and fetched 15/- to 16/-). In 1771, about 81 chests of singlo were auctioned at the Half-Moon Tavern under gradings of "good ordinary bloom, curled leaf better than common singlo and middling common singlo." Three years later the same tavern was

Silver gilt sugar bowl, Paris 1809-19, by J.B.C. Odiot

auctioning 2,115 chests of singlo along with "600 ditto in time for exportation." Singlo apparently gave more cups to the pound than the other teas, too — if you used more water — and in this sense it could be suggested that it anticipated the sort of tea-making economy that drove the British over to Indian teas a century later. For, in 1750, Dr Thomas Short, MD, recounted how people would brew tea for breakfast then strain a second helping of liquor from the same leaves and drink it in the afternoon, and another writer recommended singlo as a tea that was "strong and will endure the Change of Water three or four times."

With that sort of quality, singlo and the other lesser grades like black bohea became ideal base ingredients for concentrated tea blending which started once it was known that teas had different flavours depending on the region of origin, the types of soil in which they were grown and the state of the weather during growth. Blending accomplished a number of breakthroughs in the growth of the British tea-drinking cult. For the middle and lower classes, an ounce of expensive and coveted imperial hyson, added to a mixed pound of singlo and vulgar Green Dust could produce an acceptable grade of tea at a cheap cost, and certainly one that could be served without undue embarrassment at all but the most noble tea-tables. English cabinet makers' tea boxes of the 1730s show that whoever brewed the tea also blended it from six to eight different compartments containing various varieties.

China teas were also blended to maintain a constant standard and flavour for a market that was still largely acquiring a taste for the very idea of tea, let alone exotic blends, and this was handled initially by the East India Company's brokers, or "tasters and smellers" — one of whom "having examined in one day upwards of one hundred chests of tea, only by smelling at them forcibly ... was the next day seized with giddiness, headache, universal spasms and loss of speech and memory," and later became paralysed and died. But it was more likely a stroke, rather than the effects of tea, that killed him.

By the early 1800s, blending was done by the grocer or warehouseman for the distinctive tastes of individual clients. In 1780, John Mundy,

A typical tea sprig in close up.

proprietor of the Grasshopper in Old Broad Street, was offering "The Most Curious Superfine Gunpowder" at 16/- a lb, and in the 1800s a Ludgate Hill merchant was advertising "Club Mixture — Lovely Tea, Suitable for Five o'Clock," while a Newcastle vendor guaranteed that "Stewart's Finest Ouchain Gunpowder" would explode all prejudice against the beverage.[2] A competitor in Preston went even further with a series of advertising ditties like this one:

> *"Pure as the flake of feathery snow*
> *That floats upon the breeze;*
> *Pure as the moonbeam's radiant glow*
> *Are Dick's unequalled teas."*

The earliest and probably most celebrated blend was, and still is, Earl Grey's introduced by Jackson's of Piccadilly. According to the company this "distinct semi-scented light China flavour" — a mixture of black China tea and other grades nowadays sprayed with oil of bergamot, a citrus plant from Sicily — was a secret presented to the Victorian statesman the second Earl Grey by a mandarin at the end of a diplomatic mission to China. "This was entrusted by Lord Grey to George Charlton in 1830 — who was a partner of Robert Jackson & Co. This blend was said to be 'the perfection of Black China Tea' and 'for flavours it is unsurpassed'. Jacksons remain sole proprietors of this original formula, which remains unaltered today." Twinings dispute the claims of Jacksons and counter with the fact that they have a portrait of Earl Grey in their archives. As long ago as 1937 Jacksons announced they were selling a ton of Earl Grey's blend a week. Other Jacksons early blends included Lady

Londonderry's, Dr Milton's and Invalid, all with their special qualities and flavours."

The development and marketing invasion of Indian and then Ceylon teas led to new blendings and gradings in Britain's warehouses and retail establishments. As the quality of Indian teas improved, *broken orange pekoe* appeared on the market — referring not to the white downy tips that had characterised the Chinese pekoes, but to the golden or orange tips, looking like little chips, of the finest siftings of the Indian crops. Processors collected these by throwing siftings against sheets of hessian, to which the golden tips clung while the rest fell away. Gradually, the China names — bohea, bing, caper, singlo — gave way to the Indian gradings, with the present-day grading of black tea depending almost entirely on the size of the leaf, but not before a series of peculiar blends appeared, around the later 1800s, in which the still-inferior Indian grades were fortified with China teas. The *Art of Tea Blending*, 1884, mentioned "Mixture No. 16 (Fine), ¾ Kintuck, ¼ Ning Chow, 1/16 Foochow Pekoe, 3/16 Assam Pekoe or Orange Pekoe, ¾ Darjeeling Broken Pekoe."

In 1813, Twinings were offering no less than 13 grades of China green teas, and its China "blacks" were listed as "bohea, best congou leaf, ordinary congou, middling ditto, genuine ditto, good ditto, very good ditto, fine ditto, very fine ditto, good campoi, fine ditto, very fine ditto, good souchong, fine ditto, very

fine ditto, fine caper souchong, middling pekoe, fine ditto." Fifty years later, the grading of black teas in particular had consolidated and settled down into two classes listed in W. Hodgetts' *A Popular Treatise on Tea*: "Leaf Grades (whole leaves, as in the China Grades) — Orange Pekoe (OP) long, thin and wiry; Pekoe (P) with a shorter leaf, but giving rather more colour in the cup; Souchong (S) a broad, round leaf, and Pekoe Souchong (PS) a smaller and rougher version of the same. Broken Grades (the various sizes of broken leaves produced by sifting) — Broken Orange Pekoe (BOP); Broken Pekoe (BP); Broken Pekoe Souchong (BPS); Broken Orange Pekoe Fannings (BOFP); Dust."

Broken orange pekoe, or Golden Tips as they were called, were regarded as the cream of all the tea crops when they first appeared on the British market, particularly those from Ceylon. Though they were simply the "leaf buds of good quality tea sorted out separately (and therefore expensively) by hand, "producers and buyers built up such an inflated mystique about them that, for a short time, Golden Tips became almost worth their weight in gold. In January 1891 the precious grade went up for auction and was sold for £4.7s a lb. Through the following months, its price shot up to £17 per lb, then £25, then £30. In August, Golden Tips peaked at £36.15s a lb, and so did the one upmanship of the buyers — all of them apparently realising that madness of this sort could lead to ruin. When Golden Tips came up for sale again in December they ignored it and went back to saner, far more economical bidding. Since then, broken orange pekoe, still the finest grade to be bought, and still the most expensive, has been the essence of most tea blends. Too strong for brewing in the teapot, "Golden Tips" are now added in small amounts to

Jackson's original tea shop in London's West End.

various "lower" teas. (The Golden Tips frenzy arose again very briefly in 1937, however, when the English and Scottish Cooperative Society offered for auction teas that included glass jars containing "Superlatively Choice Golden Tip Flowery Broken Orange Pekoe of Incalculable Value from Carolina Division of Mango Range Estate)"

The introduction of packet teas, after early experimentation in the 1820s by John Horniman, is attributed to Arthur Brooke. This led to the mass marketing of teas — with Lyons, Liptons, Ty-Phoo and Co-op later joining Brooke Bonds on the grocers' shelves. Dubious trading practices arose and Arthur Brooke, for instance, had to be critically careful about his blends and the weight of his packets to triumph over a fierce public relations campaign by the bulk merchants about consumers having to foot the cost of the paper packaging; also, there were the connoisseurs and tea snobs who simply refused to have anything to do with packaged blends. "Some old fashioned retailers would still mix tea in the presence of their customers, who would taste the blends until their palates were suited. Many customers preferred to buy their tea from the original chests and mix it themselves. This practice

continued at Twinings Strand shop until about the 1930s; special canisters were kept of original

teas, the shop manager recorded the special requirements of individual customers, who were real connoisseurs."[3] On top of strong, if confined, buyer resistance, packaged teas also had to contend with unscrupulous retailers who cashed in on the craze for Ceylon teas by labelling their packets "Ceylon Tea" even though it was heavily blended with India and China grades.

As the Indian and Ceylon blends progressively dominated the package and bulk tea market in Britain, the Chinese teas fell back upon shrinking legions of loyal traditionalists and connoisseurs with a taste for exotic blends, so that in the years leading up to the beginning of this century, the vast bulk imports of hysons, gunpowders and boheas were replaced with speciality teas like "exotic scented caper" and "25 cases each containing 8 flowered and figured Red Boxes, with gold bindings and sliding lids; hand painted on each side with

tableaux from Chinese historical plays, all different (Choicest New Season's Panyong Congou.") The scented caper is another tea-producing phenomenon that may well have made the bones of old Lu Yu rattle angrily in his grave: He regarded spiced or scented teas as "no more than the swill of gutters and ditches." Today, apart from the bergamot extract (the pure oil costing about £50 per kilo) of the popular Earl Grey blend, the essence of lemon, strawberry, blackcurrant and a number of other fruits are used to scent speciality teas — sprayed into the leaves in huge revolving blending drums, the largest holding 4,000 lbs of tea at a time. The oils are very volatile, often evaporating in six months or so even in sealed containers.

Packet teas finally outstripped and indeed vanquished loose tea sales in the years leading up to World War I, and the vast majority of Britain's grocers began stocking only proprietory packets. After World War II, the retailers and smaller tea trading companies were in turn squeezed out of business by the large mass-outlet operations, with supermarkets (Tesco, for instance) joining Brooke Bond, Lyons and Co-op in a move that sidestepped the traditional London auctions and aimed at trading directly with the Indian and Ceylon tea gardens. Today, 80 percent of the tea sold at source goes to Brooke Bond, Lyons and Co-op. None of the major tea companies operating today are dealing solely in tea; with the balance of power in the tea market having shifted entirely to retailers with the support of 1,000 or so retail outlets, many of them are subsidiaries of large scale food wholesaling, and retailing, operations.

Among the oldest, most prestigious tea firms, Twinings also entered mass retailing in 1916 when it merged with the "Blend and Packet Tea Department of Messrs Harrison & Crosfield Ltd, the well known Eastern merchants," to supply teas directly to the grocery trade. It was a wise move, for the "Age of Elegance" of British society **and the tea industry disappeared**

in the thunder of two class-shattering wars. "Until the outbreak of the Second World War in 1939," the company recounts, "Twinings had a substantial direct retail trade with private families whom they had supplied for generations. Many of these customers had large country seats and kept a large staff; they used to order 25 lb, 50 lb or 100 lb of tea at a time, and a rebate was given on the quantity ordered. Those days have gone, as very few people today employ many, if any domestic staff, and it was the staff who drank the greater proportion of the tea. With customers now only requiring very small quantities for their own use ... it is now felt that it would be more beneficial to those who enjoy Twinings teas if they were able to purchase locally." Since 1964, Twinings has been part of the Associated British Food Group, along with

such companies as Ryvita, Burtons, Sunblest and ABC, and its vigorous foreign sales campaigns have been integrated with, and supported by, processed foods ranging from biscuits to frozen peas.

Jacksons, too, have had to tread forth into the mass-retail world — "leading department stores and quality food shops" throughout Britain and in 30 other countries — to retain their traditional tea business. And, like Twinings, their teas are allied with other beverages and foods. Fortnum & Mason, that blue-ribbon delicatessen-cum-department store with a history of Royal Appointments almost as long as its ledgers, has so far managed to keep its exclusive and celebrated tea blends off the supermarket and grocers' shelves and confine the sale of them to their Piccadilly premises. They, alone, have managed to retain a die-hard clientele, the sort of

Previous page: Filling tea chests at a 19th century Canton tea merchant's premises. *Above:* Testing the leaf and infusion at the modern Yingteh tea plantation in China

connoisseurs that Twinings lost to a certain extent in the 1930s — and even today, a register at the store's Tea Department counter records the special blends of F&M customers ranging from royalty to the doyens of high society, showbusiness, commerce and industry and the military. Some of their teas are the most expensive in the world. Overseas businessmen and tourists make up 75 percent to 80 percent of their tea sales. Japanese visitors have been known to take home consignments of up to six lbs of F&M tea — home to a country which is among the world's prominent tea producers. Yet, as with Twinings and Jacksons, tea is sold alongside luxury foods and a wide range of other products on the seven floors of Fortnum & Mason, including antiques, clothing, electrical goods, toys, perfumes, silverware and 'umbrellas and shooting sticks."

One common factor has kept these three traditional tea suppliers alive in a market virtually bludgeoned by the Tescos, Brooke Bonds and other giant tea retailers — speciality teas. And speciality has promoted a latter-day sophistication in the tea industry that represents yet another great revolution in the development of Lu Yu's "grand tree in the south" — tea blending.

Almost all the major brands offered for retail sale today are actually blends of between 15 and 20, sometimes 30, different teas. Rarely are absolutely pure teas marketed. Why? "For one thing, the price would be prohibitive," says Peter J. Osborn, a freelance tea blender for Jacksons and other tea retailers in London. 'When a tea is labelled, for instance, *Darjeeling* it may well be made up of about five percent pure Darjeeling, with the rest comprising what we call *price reducers* — medium quality and even low quality teas which nevertheless achieve a pure Darjeeling flavour." If the price is important — and Osborn emphasises that price considerations are dictated more by the consumer than the producer — the need for a

pleasing, distinctive and *uniform* blend of tea is absolutely cardinal. Like the addicted smoker, the dedicated tea drinker is bluntly intolerant of any change in flavour or quality of his favourite blend. In *Tea Hints for Retailers*, published in 1903, John H. Blake laid down laws which, essentially, are as religious to blenders today. "The main object of the retailer to keep in view in tea-mixing," he stated, "is to produce a tea that will please the greatest number of people; and in order to do this, *radical changes of appearance, flavour and strength must be avoided*, and a blend of teas chosen that will combine the expected drinking qualities and, at the same time, create and cause to stand out prominently in the drink a particular flavour, distinctive and yet akin to the accustomed one. To attempt to push a blend of tea composed of sufficient black varieties to make the taste of the black kinds the more pronounced, in a community accustomed to Chinese or Japanese green teas, would be folly ...."[4]

Not surprisingly, tea tasters and blenders — the best of whom are centred in London — must know everything there is to know about tea, and about as many as 30 different national and regional varieties — whether they're low, medium or fine teas and whether, for instance, they'll "marry" with each other, as Peter Osborn terms the actual blending process. Russian and China teas marry very satisfactorily. In turn, these teas can be wedded with Argentine varieties. Sidamanik Java tea has very neat leaves which can be blended with African teas. Russian, Argentine, low China types, Turkish and, at certain times, low African teas can be blended in as price reducers for Darjeeling. No more than 10 percent of a low type price reducer can be used in a blend, or it'll "come through" the flavour. The percentage of fine tea is rarely more than 15 percent, the balance made up of medium types.

Enterprising tea tasters try to get apprenticed to a prominent all-round tea dealing company

which buys and sells different teas, otherwise they run the risk of becoming limited to one particular type. There are others, no less ambitious, who prefer to specialize in one particular category of tea, and are likely to work for a large Brooke Bond type of company throughout their career, concentrating on the same blend. The Darjeeling market, according to Osborn, is one of the most important in the whole tea trade and requires blenders with a particular, esoteric expertise. Because of the demand for specialist skills, there are only perhaps 10 or 12 all-round experts, like Osborn, in Britain who can switch from blend to blend.

Whatever their particular aspirations, tasters start at the bottom of the business, making tea samples and washing up and then gradually move up through the ranks to become assistant samplers, then assistant tasters, relying at all times on knowledge and expertise handed down by the masters of the trade. They soon become fluent in the tea taster's jargon, chatting about such leaf features as *cheesy*, a smell or taint caused by inferior glue of tea-chest panels; *crepy*, crimped appearance; *grapenutty*, leaf balled in the process of manufacture; *shotty*, a well-made souchong; *whiskery*, fine hairy fibre; or they'll agree that the tea-liquor is *baggy*, tainted by hessian or sacking; *biscuity*, a pleasant characteristic; *gone off*, past its prime; *hungry*, lacking cup character; *stewed*, incorrectly fired; *sweaty*, unpleasant taste; *weedy*, thin and cabbagy. "Teas are comparable with Scotch whisky," says Peter Osborn. "The plant gives a different taste wherever it is grown, depending on the weather conditions and soil composition. You also get a different result with various waters that are used for infusion." Hence the terms *rains*, applied to North Indian teas produced during monsoons; *weathery*, an unpleasant taste on some rains teas; and, in the case of Fortnum & Mason, a once-flourishing tradition in which customers sent in samples of their drinking water so that teas

Picking, grading and drying at the Yingteh plantation.

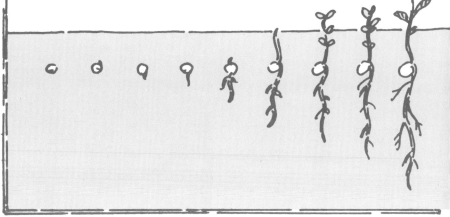

Seedlings begin a two and a half year growth to tea-producing maturity at Yingteh.

could be specially blended to match it. (F&M still advertise, as one of their speciality teas, Crown Blend — "A combination of Darjeeling and China teas. This tea was first introduced many years ago and recommended for use where a pure China tea is required with hard water.")

One of the tea industry's most eminent tasters, Stanley Dishart of Twinings, has spent over 50 years specialising in China, Darjeeling and Ceylon teas. He first joined Twinings in 1928 and spent his first five years training to develop his palate "to the point where he can not only assess the qualities and market value of any tea samples but can, by tasting the tea, determine the elevation of the tea estate on which the tea is grown and the time of year at which the leaf was plucked." It's estimated that during the fifty years up until 1978, Dishart tasted in excess of two-million samples of tea.

The palate and nose of the tea taster are as sensitively tuned as those of the wine expert, and just as carefully nursed. Most tasters do not smoke. The mouth is rinsed with warm water to make sure the palate doesn't cloy. The nose and nasal passages must be capable of detecting the slightest, most subtle fluctuations of flavour and aroma of both dry and infused tea. Though the dry leaf is mostly tested for type, grade and quality by sight and touch — an *old* tea will crumble into dust in the hand — it may also be smelled, or "nosed," with the taster breathing into the leaves to test the fragrance and categorize its blending possibilities. (Harking back to the days when the East India Company's tasters graded the teas at the warehouse, the story goes that a second broker became dizzy after testing and blending different shipments. "He was bled in the arm, an attendant had to guide his tottering steps, and finally he was 'advised to be electrified,' the shocks being directed through his head."[5] Two days later he died, though there was doubt as to whether the tea or electric shocks killed him).

Today's tasting process, as described by Peter Osborn, goes

like this: Samples of tea are prepared, each the weight of a sixpence (or two sixpences for a blending taste) in white porcelain cups with porcelain strainers and lids on them. Hot water is added and the leaves are steeped for about five minutes. When infused, the tea is strained through the strainer into a white porcelain bowl. (White china is used because it best reveals the true colour of tea). The leaves, called the *infusion*, are displayed in the strainer alongside the tea-liquor, which is called the *leaf*. The infusion is pressed with the fingers to determine the springiness of the leaf, indicating freshness and quality, then it is tested for colour, which should always be even. In the case of black teas, low quality is indicated if the infused leaves remain black or even dark. Greenish leaves are a sign that fermentation has not been completed properly. On the other hand, the infused leaves of green teas should be nothing but green, showing that no fermentation has been allowed to occur. Oolong should show green with reddish-brown edges.

Next, the infused liquor is inspected. It is smelled for aroma and examined for colour — a greenish infusion of black tea indicating poor quality or over-fermentation, and a brownish-yellow green tea betraying an old or low-grade leaf. Finally, the warm liquor is actually tasted, or rather *slurped* — the inhalation drawing a fine spray against the taster's palate and wafting the aroma up the nasal passages. The liquor must not be too hot, or the flavour cannot be accurately gauged. The tea is swilled around the mouth, sloshing back and forth over the palate, and it is here that the taster is able to compute the sample's quality in comparision with the myriad other tastes that are stored up in the sensory bank of his mind. Lastly, the tested liquor — vintage or blending treasure that it may well be — is irreverently spat into a brass spittoon.

There are other tests that have to be made — in the case of North African and some Arab consumers, whether the tea, usually a gunpowder green, will

mix nicely with mint, and whether, for most parts of the Anglo-Saxon world, the tea will retain good colour and flavour or go greyish "under the milk." The final blends themselves are again tasted and tested for quality, and, in the case of United Kingdom blends, final tasting is always with milk. Export fine teas are tasted without milk. But whatever the market, whatever the national or peculiar taste that the blender is aiming at, the guidelines that he follows and the qualities that he seeks have not changed radically from those laid down by John H. Blake in his advice to retailers almost 80 years ago:

"One of the grades or kinds, we will say, possesses delicate flavour in a marked degree; another good body; a third, aroma; a fourth strength, then the combined whole, if not interfered with by an injudiciously selected ingredient, will create a blend which will produce a drink that will have flavour, body, aroma and strength in correct and happy proportions. In such a case the qualities of each will back the others up ... and the union of all, *after assimilation*, will give a combination that will be distinctive, and yet, if carefully selected with the taste of the community in mind, not sufficiently so to be called some other kind of tea."

While the bulk tea producers concentrate on blending for mass-taste uniformity, the producers of speciality teas have transformed blending from an industry into a science — with new blends appearing year after year to suit adventurous tastes. Twinings now produce more than 60 blends of tea, 18 of which are speciality teas exported all over the world — including, of all places, tea-producing Japan where sales of Twinings tea doubled in three years up to 1976 to the tune of £3 million. Twinings' tea blending is now a technology, with 90 percent of its production taking place at an automated blending factory at Andover, Hants. But the nose and palate of the tea-taster is still the most precious component of the tea-blending chain. To quote the

Sun Yat-sen, "father" of the first Chinese Republic.

company, its tasters "sample some 500 to 800 teas a day — for to make up some blends requires more than 30 different teas, and to keep these blends constant in colour and taste needs continuous adjustment to the blend mix.

"Before a tea is ordered in quantity, the Tasting Room employs all its considerable expertise and experience on the small sample sent in by the grower's broker. The tea is checked, discussed, tasted, and finally its part in the blending plan is defined. And on the strength of that small sample, thousands of lbs of tea are bought from the far flung corners of the world — to arrive eventually, in the traditional 100 lb tea chests, at the company's large and sophisticated factories at Andover and Tyneside. To maintain the consistent quality and flavour of each blend, it is now necessary to taste the tea again. A little tea is drawn off from the consignment — what the experts in the Tasting Room do in miniature the factory will later follow in bulk. The tasters sample the carefully measured tea, checking it first in the dry form for its colour, aroma and leaf grade; and then after making tea from the sample they assess the wet leaf, and the colour and taste of the liquor. The blending plan is tested and approved.

"Now automation takes over. The tea is blended in one of four large drums, each with a capacity of 3,000 lbs. The operation is controlled by one person operating a console table. The tea enters a blending drum ... for a predetermined length of time; then the tea is discharged into mobile hoppers. These hoppers are taken to the floor above the packing halls and gravity fed, according to the production plan, into the appropriate machines either (to) be made up into packets or tins or into one of a series of intriguing and intricate machines which packs them into tea bags."

Among the Darjeelings, Keemun and Lapsang Souchongs, Uva Ceylons, Lemon Scented Teas and all the other orthodox and speciality blends that Twinings produce, the most popular is its version of the "secret" Earl Grey. Jackson's still command a strong domestic and export position with their own Earl Grey, which is described thus: "the blend having remained unchanged for more than 140 years. It is the delight of tea lovers everywhere whose taste is for a delicately scented tea with mild flavour"; and they're offering a range of 12 other India, Ceylon, China and even Russian blends that include such romantic delights as "Ching Wo

Left: High-grown tea bushes in India take up to 10 years to mature.

— This delicately scented tea is not often seen outside China. It is grown deep in the province of Fukien, where few Europeans have ever penetrated. Connoisseurs of the exotic East will particularly appreciate Ching Wo tea, which is best drunk with a slice of lemon" and "Russian Tea — This tea is grown in the foothills of the Caucasian mountains near the border between Russia and Turkey. It is long leafed and has a character and appearance not unlike some of the teas from China. It is best drunk with a slice of lemon."

Fortnum & Mason offer a total of 24 expensive pure and blended teas (including Earl Grey) ranging from "Pure Assam, Golden Orange Broken Pekoe — A bold tea of exceptional distinction" to "Pure Darjeeling-F/M Broken Orange Pekoe Extra — An outstanding special grade of tea with a most delicious muscat flavour" to "Mandarin Pekoe — A Jasmine-scented 'Honoured Guest' Chinese tea of greenish Character. A delicate and pale afternoon tea" and "Fortmason Blend — A Russian style blend of China and Indian teas specially scented by Fortnum & Mason to serve with lemon."

Blending has indeed been the 20th century phenomenon of the history and development of tea. There are today no less than 1,500 different blends of tea for the world to choose from, with another as yet unestimated range of scented teas. And they all come from the latter-day trimmed, nursed and carefully nurtured descendents of Lu Yu's "grand tree in the south."

Yingteh plantation at harvest time — "The hills are full of girls picking tea/They carry baskets and pick from the east side to the west/They are laughing."

The Plant and The Processes

There is, in fact, a tea tree in Yunnan, southwestern China, which is 800 years old, is three feet wide at its lowest trunk and stands 60 feet high. It still produces good tea, and workers climb to the top to pick the youngest and best leaves. But much has changed with the tea tree since Lu Yu's day. Primarily, it is now a bush, constantly trimmed to an average height of between four and six feet in an evolving cultivation process that has made it more convenient for plucking — for there is no machine as nimble and selective as the human hand — and increased the number of yields, or "flushes," that can be taken from it each season. Whilst Lu Yu haughtily judged wild tea the best, with garden tea taking second place, today it is the cultivated plant of the world's tea gardens and plantations that serves the world's tea tables.

The tea plant, called *Camellia sinensis* and now categorised as a flowering evergreen shrub, can grow just about anywhere in the world, but produces commercial crops only in tropical and subtropical areas. And even here, it flourishes best in a jungle atmosphere of continual heat and humidity and produces its finest teas on hillsides over 5,000 feet above sea-level. Though the plant's mature leaves grow from one to 12 inches in length, the best teas — the pekoe tip and flowery pekoes — come from the "tiny young shoots and their thin, unopened buds."[6] The youngest leaf that has opened next to the leaf bud produces orange pekoe. The next youngest leaf gives the standard pekoe, and then, with the older, coarser leaves closer to the trunk of the shrub, come the souchongs and lesser and lower grades. Bushes grown on low tropical plains take about two and a half years to three years to mature and produce tea crops, and may produce flushes — the tender young leaves from which the tea is made — every fortnight or so during the hot season. On Hainan Island, off the southern coast of China, bushes can be

plucked up to 11 months of the year. In subtropical and temperate areas the number of flushes per year, and plucking months, decrease as the climate gets cooler. High-grown hill bushes take up to 10 years to mature, but because the cooler climate slows growth the bushes produce richer, finer grades of leaf. But whether *Camellia sinensis* is high grown, as on the Himalayan slopes of Darjeeling, or cultivated in the steamy lowland Sam Sui (Three Waters) delta opening into the South China Sea, it has a common tea-producing lifespan of 60 years or more.

Nearly all tea is plucked by human hand, and in almost all tea-producing countries the job is done by women and girls, whose fingers are the most nimble. With baskets on their backs they move slowly through the green, neatly pruned lanes of waist-high foliage picking only the terminal bud and two top leaves of each bush's new flush. In India, a skilled plucker can gather about 66 to 77 lbs of green leaf in one day, sufficient to produce about 17 to 20 lbs of manufactured black tea. In the days of the British Raj, working conditions were harsh. Pluckers and processors served long apprenticeships on subsistence wages and were arrested if they tried to leave their plantation. Cheap labour meant low prices, and with tea and bread becoming the mainstay of the British industrial worker's diet, prices had to be kept low. In the Assam plantations, cholera was rife and thousands of workers imported from the slums of Calcutta suffered a miserable working life — their first hardships being a fever-ridden trek through the Ganges delta to get to the high-country estates. It wasn't until the 1880s that the British companies instituted adequate transport, with steamers shipping the labourers from Calcutta. India's independence and the formation of tea industry unions have vastly improved the working conditions, however, with today's pickers and processors commanding wages higher than those of the national average for labourers. But Ceylon (Sri Lanka), which

Tea gatherers in southern China.

practically lives off tea (it accounts for something like 70 percent of the country's total export revenue), has only recently begun raising the wages and conditions of its 500,000 or so tea plantation labourers — many of them Tamils from South India — above the subsistence level that has existed since the British first opened up the plantations with indentured labour in the 1870s.

Since nationalisation of Sri Lanka's tea industry in sweeping land reforms brought in after 1972, the country's estimated 600,000 acres of plantation have been supervised by 20 different authorities that are now supervised by the Estates Development Board and Plantations Ministry. Price-related wage supplements have been granted to field hands and new pay scales instituted for management and office staff. In a 15-year "master plan" launched with the support of the World Bank, World Food Programme, UNICEF and Canadian and Norwegian aid, new housing is to be built for plantation workers and "the degrading 'line rooms'," a hangover from British times, (restructured) into more roomy twin cottages .... Educational and voting facilities and local government voting rights will be brought in along national lines removing discriminations against estate labour. Expectant mothers and children below five years will be able to obtain free milk and 150 creches, adequately equipped and staffed, will be set up each year."[7]

If those are the sort of labour reforms planned for the future, it's not difficult to imagine how bad conditions were in the past. But even today, figures on tea plantation wages are either not mentioned or are the hardest to find in the masses of production, marketing and consumption charts and statistics released each year. India keeps the best records at the tail-end of its annual *Tea Statistics*, setting out the average daily wage for plantation workers in each main tea-producing region, along with food concessions, production bonuses and cost of living adjustments. So far as Sri Lanka is concerned, in

1972 the average daily wage of a plantation worker was 1½ rupees, with a special allowance of another 1.6 rupees for "members of the Employees Provident Fund." Today, the average plantation worker in North India gets about 4 rupees a day — that's the equivalent of US$0.44. It is known that Sri Lankan rates are generally lower than those in India, and that the Sri Lankan rupee is worth half its Indian counterpart anyway. All in all, it's true to say that the power of the tea industry still relies on basic labour that is, by Western standards, appallingly cheap.

Both the Sri Lankans and the Japanese have, in fact, experimented with tea-plucking machines, but in both cases the mechanical pickers failed (though machines are still used alongside handpicking in Taiwan). The Japanese ended up with too many stalks in their harvests, and in Sri Lanka the method made "little progress" because, as a London Ceylon Tea Centre publication points out "the main problem is that machines do not have the same ability as human beings to select the correct shoots for plucking. It should be emphasised too, that as long as tea estates continue to be more or less self-contained units, consisting of families with a high birth rate, it is more a question of providing work and food for these ever-increasing numbers rather than of making a drastic reduction in hand labour."[8]

Tea estates, forming the sort of vast regional plantations that are a feature of India and Sri Lanka, are another contemporary development of the tea industry, a product of 19th century British industriousness in India and a successor in Sri Lanka to sprawling, long-established coffee plantations that were destroyed by blight in the early 1800s. Up until that time, tea, native only to China and Japan (though transplanted on a relatively minor scale in Java), was grown in tea *gardens* — or "little shrubberies of evergreens, dotted upon the sides of all the hills," as the intrepid Robert Fortune described them after infiltrating China in *mufti* in 1843. Another observer of the times, a Miss Gordon-Cumming, waxed poetically about tea-gardens cultivated by Buddhist monks and Taoist priests in the Bohea mountains — home of the high grade black tea of the same name — between Kiangsi and Fukien provinces. Recounting how many of their monasteries and temples were "perched on summits of perpendicular precipices which, seen from the river below, appear to be wholly inaccessible," she went on to describe how "the tea-gardens where these agricultural brethren toil so diligently are most irregular patches of ground of every size and shape, scattered here, there and everywhere among these rocky mountains, but, like all Chinese gardening, tea-cultivation is exquisitely neat and the multitude of curiously clipped little bushes have a curiously formal appearance in contrast with the reckless manner in which nature has tossed about the fragments of her shattered mountains."

At the turn of this century, with Indian and Ceylon teas having virtually swept the Chinese products from the huge British market, the Chinese tea-grower was still diligently tilling the soil of what was essentially a little plot rather than a large, organised commercial undertaking. Tea-plantations in China were, wrote Blake in 1903, "in the most part unworthy of the name, for they are rarely more than little patches of the shrub, cared for by small farmers who raise and cultivate the plants, pick and partially cure the leaves and, in this condition, sell them to the travelling factors or 'tea-men' who are sent out by the 'hong' or tea-factory owners of the local interior cities. The entire farm of many Chinese tea-growers is quite frequently of such small extent that it would hardly suffice to make an ordinary house-orchard for a prosperous American farmer. Upon this little patch, however, John Chinaman grows his crop of tea-leaves and, in addition, manages to raise a sufficiency of garden-truck upon which to support his family."[9]

The "plantations" of Japan weren't much bigger; they were mostly "little spots of land cultivated by the owners. In the larger tea-districts of the country many of these tea-gardens adjoin and, spreading away over the gently rolling land, frequently by the side of the yellow-green rice fields, present, in summer, an exceedingly pleasant aspect, with their foliage of dark-green, especially if the picture is still further enlivened by women and children in their gay, clean clothes, busily picking the leaves."

But the Japanese tea industry was expanding, and on an industrial scale, whereas tea-growing in China remained in its traditional gardens — producing traditional teas — until successive waves of revolution and war rolled over them. Japan was opening up new land to tea, and the "light body and delicate flavour" of its green teas and semi-fermented oolongs was becoming widely accepted in a market opened up by Commodore Perry's gunboat diplomacy of 1854 — the United States and Canada. In 1902, Japan was a serious rival to China's tea trade; while China's tea exports to Britain had tumbled from 150-million lbs to 15-million lbs, China teas were also having to compete with Japan's in the North American market. In a single year, China's exports to America fell by 20 million lbs to 30 million lbs, and although they doubled again the next year, largely because of abnormal buying, they faced a growing Japanese export threat that in 1902 stood at 34 million lbs. One reason for the slide in China's tea trade was given by the US Consul in Shanghai in 1901, who complained about "increasing carelessness of preparation" of China teas. Thereafter, the quality and export production of China's tea industry reeled under the successive shock-waves of Sun Yat-sen's republican overthrow of the Manchu rulers, civil war triggered by a subsequent Kuomintang revolution, Japanese military incursion from Manchuria, World War II and finally the bloody internecine struggle that culminated in the communist victory in 1949.

Meanwhile, the industrial revolution of tea, marked by the establishment of large-scale tea plantations, had been spreading around the world. The Japanese had planted tea in Formosa (Taiwan), opening up an industry which now covers some 85,000 acres of land, with individual plantations as big as 2,500 acres or more. Taiwan has since been producing about 40 different types of tea and has built up an unrivalled reputation for its fruity, semi-fermented oolongs. Large tea plantations had also been set up by the British in Africa, in Malawi (then Nyasaland) in 1886, in Uganda in 1900, in Kenya in 1904 and Tanzania in the 1920s. Teas from these huge African estates — a total 1.3 million acres under cultivation in Kenya alone — have lately been challenging Sri Lankan teas, which, though increasing in production in recent years, have lost a lot of their traditional quality since nationalisation. In fact, there were indications in 1978, according to the *Far Eastern Economic Review*, that "Sri Lanka's traditional buyers, notably Australia, had expressed concern about the decline in quality, a fall attributable to the poor management of properties vested in the State after land reform. Earlier standards of tea manufacturing and administrative efficiency deteriorated badly. In the tea price boom (1976-77) the new managements sacrificed quality for quantity on the premise that anything could be sold in a situation in which world tea stocks were low and consumer demand very firm."[10]

Kenya's teas, in particular, are now regarded as first class, largely through expansion, modernisation and new production methods introduced after World War II. And the industry is still expanding, with new plantations laid out over the past few years.

In this shifting, fluctuating power-play within the global tea industry, China is now bursting back into the top ranks of the tea-exporting field. Its industry has been consolidated, its production methods modernised, its teas vastly improved in quality and variety, its marketing streamlined through the Tea Export Corporation which has its headquarters in Peking and branches in all major southern cities and tea-producing centres and is now exporting to almost 100 countries of the world. Most important of all, China has joined the "plantation club" — its "little patches of shrub" and individual tea gardens now replaced by huge, strictly disciplined Chinese versions of the Indian and Sri Lankan estates, the tea communes, or, more realistically profit-basis state enterprise.

The Yingteh tea plantation, about 100 miles north of Canton, is a good example of the sort of revolution that has taken place in China's tea industry in a bid to regain its old supremacy on the world market. Opened up around 1956 with seedlings transplanted from Yunnan, the Yingteh commune is a grouping of 12 sub-plantations and five processing factories — the largest plant, the Red Banner factory, aiming for an eventual production of 500 tons of tea a year. This whole commune, with a total workforce of around 16,000 people, with its own schools, hospitals, hydro-electricity, building materials and foodstuffs, with well over 20,000 tea bushes either producing tea or nearing maturity, with its own research institute currently experimenting with 17 new species of tea, covers an area no less than 25 miles long. Already noted for its broken black teas, the Yingteh plantation is perfecting one particular variety which could well lead to yet another radical shift of power in the world tea industry — an Assam-type leaf with which China obviously hopes to mount an attack on the citadels of Indian and Sri Lankan exports.

At this point in the story of tea, a clear and common picture emerges of today's vast plantations, wherever in the world they may be, and the common pattern of colours that their daily operations present — swelling seas and soaring waves of green amid which the tea-pluckers wade, the whole gentle, unchanging rhythm of man and nature lyricised — romantically, perhaps — by the "Tea Picking Song" from China's Fukien province:

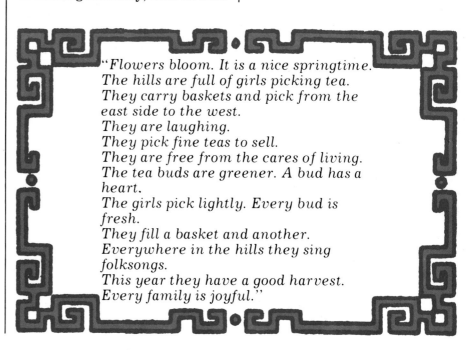

"*Flowers bloom. It is a nice springtime.*
The hills are full of girls picking tea.
They carry baskets and pick from the east side to the west.
They are laughing.
They pick fine teas to sell.
They are free from the cares of living.
The tea buds are greener. A bud has a heart.
The girls pick lightly. Every bud is fresh.
They fill a basket and another.
Everywhere in the hills they sing folksongs.
This year they have a good harvest.
Every family is joyful."

After poetry like that, the actual processing of the tea into its three basic types — green, black and oolong — is a comparatively mundane, technical affair that takes place in the factory sheds. Again, the process is common to all tea-producing areas, though machinery may differ from country to country, and follows three basic rules: green tea is unfermented, oolong is partly fermented and the blacks go through a full fermentation process. Fermentation, or oxidation, gives the leaf its bright coppery colour, converts the aroma into its characteristic fruity one and gives the liquor that rich strength that the British like their teaspoons to stand upright in. Production of green tea virtually requires only that the prime buds be steamed or fired (steamed in Japan, India and Sri Lanka, fired in ovens in China) to sterilize the leaves and arrest fermentation, then rolled in machines which curl the leaves and bring out the full flavour. From there, they are dried, then machine-graded for style (the tea-taster defines the actual market value later) and packed. Oolong teas are spread out on trays in the factory or the open sun and allowed to wilt in a process in which they absorb oxygen and the resultant chemical change liberates the tea oils that give them their distinctive fragrance and rich, spicy flavours. Fermentation is allowed to reach about 70 percent in Taiwan, today's most celebrated producer of oolongs, then the process is quickly arrested by rolling and firing. The Taiwanese also produce a mid-range tea called *pouchang* in which the fermentation process is stopped at 30 percent. Black teas go the whole road, through about six different production processes described in easy layman's terms by the Tea Council publication *How Tea is Grown and Manufactured*:

"The first phase of manufacturing is *withering*. The plucked leaf is spread on racks or troughs where, in the course of 24 hours at a temperature of 25 to 30°C, withering reduces moisture in the leaves which makes them limp. In the second phase of manufacture, the withered leaf is put through *rolling* machines, which break up the cells, thus releasing the natural juices and enzymes which give tea its characteristic flavour. The leaf also gets torn and twisted at this stage. (A variation in processing is CTC, or *Legge-cut*, manufacture. With this process, the withered leaf is lightly rolled without pressure, the fine leaf is separated and the other leaf fed into a special machine which cuts, tears and curls it.) *Fermentation* is the third phase. The leaf is spread on trays, slabs or troughs in a cool, humid atmosphere which in one to three hours oxidises the leaf and turns it to a bright coppery colour through the absorption of oxygen. After fermentation the leaf is dried by the *firing* process, during which trays of leaf move slowly through hot air chambers. The leaf now turns dark brown or black. In the final phase, the dry black leaves are sorted into various *grades* by sifting machines which vibrate them through meshes of different size into various containers, from which the tea chests are subsequently filled."

There are differences in some phases of the process, depending on tradition and technology — in China's Yingteh factories, for instance, black tea is sifted into grades in an airshaft which blows the leaf across a series of funnels, the largest leaves travelling the least distance and the smallest broken pieces, the "fannings," collecting at the end of the machine. But, basically, that's how tea is produced, whether it be in India, Sri Lanka, China or Kenya.

The refinements of various national products are far more exotic. In China and Taiwan, dried jasmine, chrysanthemums, roses, gardenias, orchids and peppermint are added to some processed teas, particularly the oolongs and pouchung, for special flavouring. The Chinese also scent some of their black teas with the essence of lichee, roses and tangerines. Earl Grey and lemon-scented teas have already been mentioned. Pine wood is another subtle flavouring added to China black teas. In fact, while India and Ceylon dominate the tea industry in terms of production and export, China remains the world's treasure-house of distinctive, speciality types; there are literally hundreds of them.

Of the green teas the fragrant *Heung Pin*, jasmine tea, literally translated as Fragrant Leaves, is the international favourite. Varieties like Silver Needle have small pointed leaves, *Chiao She Hao* and *Chung Feng* have larger leaves and more jasmine flowers in them. *Lung Ching*, or Dragon Well, named after a spring near Hangchow, is considered the very best green tea in China. Extra fine Lung Ching has a

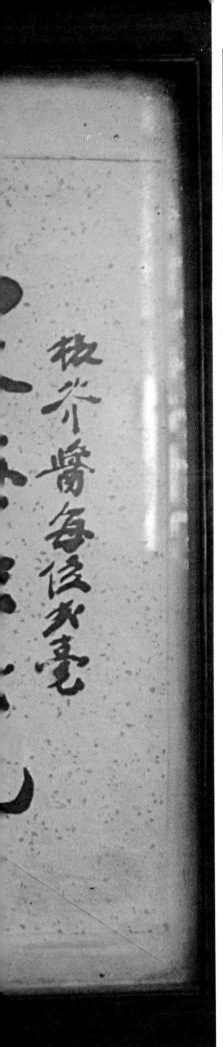

medium-sized flattish leaf and is expensive, at around $4 an ounce. *Sao Mei, Low Hon, Woo Lung* and *Siu Sin* (Water Lily) are all light, tantalyzing and popular green teas, while *Cloud Mist* is a highly regarded green tea grown in the mountains of Kiangsi where, legend has it — and the intrepid Robert Fortune is alleged to have actually witnessed it — monkeys were trained to pluck the leaves from the most inaccessible heights. There are rare and costly green teas which the Chinese call *white*, like *Ching Cha* and *Bak Mou Tan* (White Peony), whose leaves are said to be gently caressed by the human hand to extract the oils during processing. White Peony is currently on sale in some Hong Kong herbalist shops at around $12 an ounce. Another special green tea is *Pi Lo Chun* (Hair of the Girl) which is grown in cool conditions around Soochow and has a very fine small leaf. Otherwise, the "trade" range of Chinese greens are marketed, particularly for export, under the traditional gradings — hyson, gunpowder etc.

Oolongs are much appreciated by the Chinese. The nationalists of Taiwan market something like 40 different varieties — including the greener pouchangs — the most famous of which is *Tung Ding* from Luku (Deer Valley) in the mountains of central Taiwan. In the mainland People's Republic, an excellent oolong is *Tit Koon Yum* (Iron Goddess of Mercy), a favourite of the Chiu Chow (Chinese around Amoy and marketed under names like *Tit Koon Yum* and *Tit Kuan Yin*. The Chiu Chows serve their oolongs very strong in thimble-sized cups at the beginning and end of their meals. In a weaker infusion it is popular with the Cantonese *dim sum* tea-lunches. Both the types mentioned above are superlative oolongs and range in price from $8 to $20 a lb. *Tit Koon Yum* is the most costly, and rarest of the lot, and, in its finest form, something that only the true connoisseur would buy. It is said that the best comes from one peak of one single mountain in Fukien, facing the south.

Black teas, less refined in

quality and flavour except for the very finest orange pekoes, are not widely favoured by the Chinese — and perhaps that's the most essential reason why China lost her rich tea trade with Britain. However, as the production of the Yingteh tea plantation illustrates, black teas are China's most important exports today and broken orange pekoes are now being produced which are aimed at rivalling Assam teas. On the domestic side, the southern Chinese — mainly those of Kwangtung province — have for ages shown a fondness for a dark and smoky black tea known as *Bo Lay* (usually marketed as *Po Erh*), the best of which is grown in Yunnan province. An unusual black tea is *Liu Pao*, red in the cup and with a tang reminiscent of betal nut. *Chiny Wu* from Fukien is another black which produces a clear reddish infusion and has excellent body and fragrance. Main feature of the newcomer to the range, Yingteh black tea, is its strong, spicy and astringent liquor — a fresh, bright tea which takes milk well. China's two biggest export black teas are *Kee Mun* (Lion Mountain), named after the district in Anhwei province where it is grown and described as having "the fragrance of an orchid," and *Lapsang Souchong*, with its large and more brittle leaf, which has a pungent smoky or tarry flavour due to the soil in which it is grown and the fact that it is one of the teas permeated with pine wood smoke during processing.

The award for the most exotic of Chinese teas must go to one called *Ho Chin* (Hair Point), an antique now found only in brick form, costing a small fortune and used mainly for its medicinal value. This tea was made, according to one connoisseur, from the tiniest young buds just off the shoot and then sold in small cane baskets worn over the breasts of young girls who sat in tea shops to entice custom. Their body warmth matured the leaves, which came to be known as Fragrance of a Young Girl Tea.

India's 10,000 tea plantations are said to produce over 1,000

A menu from Lok Yu teahouse, Hong Kong.

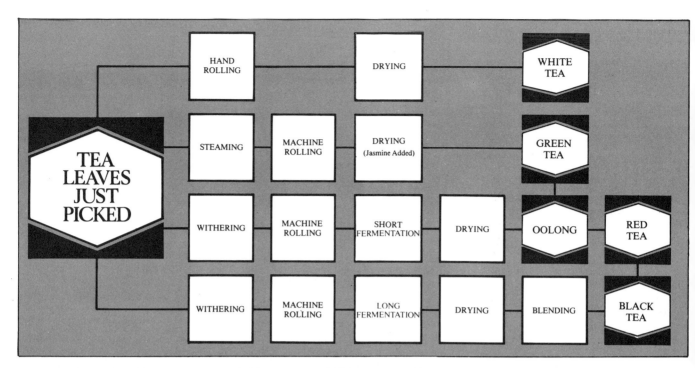

```
                    ┌──────────┐        ┌──────────┐        ╱────────╲
                    │   HAND   │────────│  DRYING  │────────│ WHITE  │
                    │ ROLLING  │        │          │        │  TEA   │
                    └──────────┘        └──────────┘        ╲────────╱

╱──────────╲        ┌──────────┐  ┌──────────┐  ┌──────────┐  ╱────────╲
│   TEA    │        │          │  │ MACHINE  │  │  DRYING  │  │ GREEN  │
│  LEAVES  │────────│ STEAMING │──│ ROLLING  │──│(Jasmine  │──│  TEA   │
│   JUST   │        │          │  │          │  │ Added)   │  ╲────────╱
│  PICKED  │        └──────────┘  └──────────┘  └──────────┘
╲──────────╱
          │    ┌──────────┐  ┌──────────┐  ┌──────────┐  ┌──────────┐  ╱────────╲  ╱────────╲
          │    │          │  │ MACHINE  │  │  SHORT   │  │  DRYING  │  │ OOLONG │  │  RED   │
          ├────│WITHERING │──│ ROLLING  │──│FERMENTA- │──│          │──│        │──│  TEA   │
          │    │          │  │          │  │  TION    │  │          │  ╲────────╱  ╲────────╱
          │    └──────────┘  └──────────┘  └──────────┘  └──────────┘

          │    ┌──────────┐  ┌──────────┐  ┌──────────┐  ┌──────────┐  ┌──────────┐  ╱────────╲
          │    │          │  │ MACHINE  │  │   LONG   │  │  DRYING  │  │ BLENDING │  │ BLACK  │
          └────│WITHERING │──│ ROLLING  │──│FERMENTA- │──│          │──│          │──│  TEA   │
               │          │  │          │  │  TION    │  │          │  │          │  ╲────────╱
               └──────────┘  └──────────┘  └──────────┘  └──────────┘  └──────────┘
```

varieties of mainly black, and some green teas, most of them identified with the district in which they're grown or whether they're fine, medium or low grades in the complicated blending processes which take place in the Indian capital cities for domestic consumption, on the one hand, and in London for the British market and re-export. To make a potentially long story short, the most popular Indian and Sri Lankan types can be listed as *Assam*: A strong Indian tea with a rich, warm, pungent flavour; *Darjeeling*: A world famous tea noted for its rich and exquisite bouquet; *Nilgiri*: A light tea with a delicate flavour grown in the Nilgiri hills in Southern India. In Sri Lanka — *Dimbula*: A typical fine-flavoured, golden-coloured high grown tea from plantations 5,000 feet or more above sea level; *Nuwara Eliya* (pronounced New-ray-lia). A delicate tea famous for its light, bright colour and fragrant flavour; *Uva*: A fine-flavoured tea grown on the eastern slopes of the Central Mountains.

With China's tea industry bidding again for world leadership, the next few decades should see a battle royal between its black teas and those of India and Sri Lanka, with those of Kenya mounting their own simultaneous marketing assault. China has already regained its dominance in the green tea market and is driving forcefully into the United States now that the China Trade Embargo of the fifties and early sixties has been dropped. With the normalisation of relations with America, China

should soon monopolise the US market altogether. As far as the lucrative British trade is concerned, China's Tea Export Corporation is sidestepping the traditional auctions and dealing directly with the major tea suppliers — selling two million lbs of speciality teas a year to Twinings, for example, along with its black teas which Twinings are blending into a product called China Black and

which caused *Vintage Magazine* to declare in its August, 1973 edition: "Welcome back real Chinese tea!" Chinese tea exports to Britain are now running at between 16 million and 20 million lbs a year.

Meanwhile, a new Indian tea has appeared on the British market. It is called Runglee Rungliot of Darjeeling. And it is strong and bitter.

im sum' (little delicacies) *left*; tea chests and kettles *right*.

The exo

"Nearly 3,000 feet up a mountain in Wales. Misty, bitterly cold, desolate. Heavens above! Man inside hut brewing and selling hot, strong Indian tea. Thick cups, no saucers. What nectar!"

That terse, but nonetheless worshipful record of the ecstacy of tea came not from the diary of some bearded, grizzled expedition leader or an ex-India Army mountaineer. It came from Mrs Ivy Potts of Pinner, in Middlesex, and won her a £10 grocery voucher for every week for a year and a £200 cash prize in a competition organised in 1973 by *Good Housekeeping* and sponsored by Twinings and Chinacraft.

Thousands of British housewives took part in the contest, the rules of which required them to take seven blends of Twinings teas, Earl Grey, Lapsang Souchong, Keemun, Ceylon, Darjeeling, Orange Pekoe and Assam, and match them with seven social events and menus in the home. As a tie-breaker, in case more than one entrant came up with the right answers, each had to recount an unusual occasion when a cup of tea was really appreciated. No-one could beat Mrs Potts' ecstacy amid ordeal, but Mrs Kate Chester came very close with a story about her tiring journey to a christening when she was godmother to the child. "To my amazement after the service, a curtain at the side of the altar was drawn back to reveal a boiling kettle and a cup of tea was offered. An answer to a prayer? Blend of Darjeeling, Assam and Ceylon."

Such odes in praise of tea have

Porcelain "cat" teapot, 19th century, Foshan Monastery, Kwangtung.

90

been sounding for centuries — whether pencilled in on the dotted line of a promotion coupon, painted in thick black characters on a Chinese scroll or simply bayed at the moon by tea-inebriated troubadors. Such has been the mystique, the *exotica*, that has, like the rising voice of a choir, swelled up in holy adoration of tea since the father of tea himself, Lu Yu, first got slightly beside himself with praise. Apologising for the "vulgarity" of describing tea-leaves as shrinking and crinkling "like a Mongol's boots (or) the dewlap of a wild ox," Lu then flew to the very edge of poetic licence in his description of tea's "myriad of shapes."

"It can look like a mushroom in whirling flight just as clouds do when they float out from behind a mountain peak. Its leaves can swell and leap as if they were being lightly tossed on wind-disturbed water. Still others will twist and turn like the rivulets carved out by a violent rain in newly tilled fields."

Less poetic, yet no less inspired, was the waltz song "Lewis's Beautiful Tea" composed some 1,200 years later in Britain to promote a cheap department store blend. Denys Forrest writes: "Its elegant cover was familiar to me for many years before I ever heard it performed, but in 1859 a 'Talking Teapot' actually sang it to visitors to a Ceylon Tea Exhibition in the Manchester store."[1] Though there's no record to hand of the words of that particular song, the tone, if not the essence, of Britain's 19th-century tributes to tea can be gauged from the lyrics *The Cup for Me*, penned by an anonymous tea-addict in 1899:

White glazed porcelain, English (Chelsea), about 1745-50.

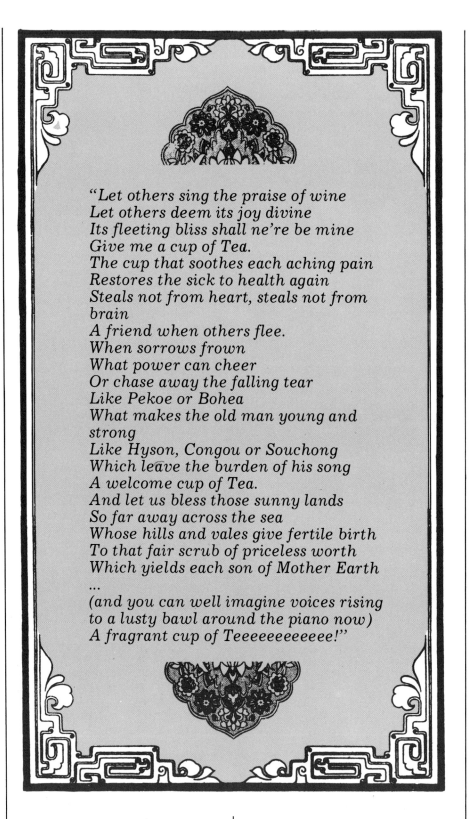

"Let others sing the praise of wine
Let others deem its joy divine
Its fleeting bliss shall ne're be mine
Give me a cup of Tea.
The cup that soothes each aching pain
Restores the sick to health again
Steals not from heart, steals not from brain
A friend when others flee.
When sorrows frown
What power can cheer
Or chase away the falling tear
Like Pekoe or Bohea
What makes the old man young and strong
Like Hyson, Congou or Souchong
Which leave the burden of his song
A welcome cup of Tea.
And let us bless those sunny lands
So far away across the sea
Whose hills and vales give fertile birth
To that fair scrub of priceless worth
Which yields each son of Mother Earth
...
(and you can well imagine voices rising
to a lusty bawl around the piano now)
A fragrant cup of Teeeeeeeeeeee!"

Heady stuff, but amid all the hymns of worship and praise, the celebration of tea was lifted to even loftier heights when a shower of handbills inscribed PRIORY TEA — BEST VALUE IN THE WORLD! was "dropped from the skies by Lieut. Lemprière, navigating the Golden Eagle Balloon, June 16th, 1894." And for another example of Britain's passion and reverence for the beverage, this one some 50 years later, consider the account of Lord Woolton, Minister of Food during the Battle of Britain in World War II, who stated: "When London was being persistently bombed, I had to tell the tea blenders to remove their stocks to less vulnerable positions." Lord Woolton also recounted how, because of dwindling wartime supplies, the pooling of tea was considered, the idea being to create one common brand so that everyone would get some. Woolton fiercely resisted the scheme, and later proudly reported that "fortunately the result justified the conclusion. If we had given up during the war the blending of tea, the use of brands, if we had decided on this dull level of equality, we should have lost something in our national life ... Taste, individual taste, is worth preserving and cultivating; it adds to the joy of living and flavours existence."

The joy that was Britain's had, by then, long been a religion and an art in the two cradles of the tea industry, China and Japan. In China, the early cultivation of tea required that seeds be watered with the same water in which rice had been washed, that the seedlings be planted near a stand of bamboo or under a mulberry tree on which silkworms fed and that the maidens who picked the tea bathe every morning before setting out for the fields and, for three weeks before plucking, abstain from eating fish and certain meats so that their breath might not affect the bouquet of the leaves. (Much later, at the turn of this century, John H. Blake noted that tea-growers in the coastal districts of Japan were manuring their gardens with fish-guano, oil-cake and "other strong-smelling fertilizers" and these were responsible for the "fishy" flavour of many of the lower grades of Japan teas.[2])

By the time of China's Sung dynasty, Wu Tzu-mu was declaring that the essentials that "people cannot do without every day are firewood, rice, oil, salt, soybean sauce, vinegar and tea." In the Ming dynasty, the Empress and her consorts presented daily offerings to the imperial forebears, and on the first day of each moon, rolled fried cakes were laid out, on the second finely granulated sugar and on the third day, tea from eastern Szechuan, regarded as the birthplace of China's teas. Tea had earned an essential role in religion, superstition and custom. Boat people — the fishing families who lived, worked and died aboard floating "townships" of junks and sampans — included ceremonial teas in their wedding festivities. Red packets containing tea were used, along with fruit and flowers, to dress their temple altars; and the tea was presented as a palliative and healing agent to worshippers as they left the shrines. For the dead, it was believed that tea eased the path through purgatory. "In the seventh week after death the soul enters the realm of the Prince of the Wheel, and there petitions to expedite its transmigration. A rest house provides tea for it. A virtuous soul finds the tea comforting, cool and refreshing. An evil-doer can only expect the tea to erase all memory of his past."[3] In the Festival of the Hungry Ghosts, still observed annually by the Cantonese, tea is an important element, along with rice, vegetables, incense and symbolic gold and silver paper, of rituals aimed at appeasing neglected or mischievous ghosts that might take it upon themselves to haunt the community in the year ahead.

As a medicine, the Chinese used tea to alleviate rheumatism and stimulate blood circulation and, as the pharmacology of tea became better known, applied it as a digestive — jasmine tea, in particular, renowned for helping "sufferers of frequent, acute stomach aches" — and a cure for colds. Green tea blended with chrysanthemums was used to soothe the liver, relax the nerves and brighten the eyes. A contemporary report on teas and herbal medicines in Taiwan mentions that "chrysanthemum tea, ti ku lu, which literally means dew of the earth's bone, is drunk more for its medicinal properties than for its taste. It's a colourless brew with a strong herbal aroma which many have found distasteful. Most people who drink it add a little honey to pick up its flavour. But ti ku lu is said to be most efficacious in dispersing the body's heat, a basic step in summer health care. In addition, because the Chinese believe that a person is bound to

contract intermittent fever if he does not perspire during the summer, they drink ti ku lu to stimulate perspiration. It is recommended especially for people who have just had surgical operations because it is a mild medicine and can be easily absorbed by a weak constitution. It is also drunk as a restorative by people who have been out in the sun for a long time or who have exerted themselves excessively."

In an early practice which perhaps foreshadowed the mammoth tea-guzzling temperance cult of 19th-century Britain, the Chinese are said to have used tea to combat alcoholism. "A Chinese gentleman in the 5th century observed that tea leaves, when they fell into pools, left an orange tinge and bitter taste. After tasting it he dismissed it as too acrid to drink. Then it occurred to him that it might discourage alcoholism. His method was simply to drown his patient internally with it. 'If I keep him full of this harsh stuff,' he reasoned, 'he will have no room for alcohol.' The cure worked."[4] (Anyone with a concise knowledge of the causes and effects of alcoholism would argue, however, that a treatment like that would more likely drive the patient closer to drink, rather than away from it).

Anyway, the medicinal qualities of tea were not ignored by contemporary physicians when the beverage became common in the West. Amid the loud squabble that raged on whether tea was a harmless stimulant or a sin, one British

doctor quietly observed that "tea, if not drunk too hot nor in too great quantities, is perhaps preferable to any other vegetable infusion," and at the turn of the 20th century it was the opinion of another physician that denying tea to a sick person might do more harm than good. "A rather weak tea (never a strong one) may be made of any of the ordinary green or black teas, when craved by the sick, sweetening and using milk as desired; for we believe it better to allow a mild beverage of this kind to any sick person rather than to allow their minds to worry over a refusal, for all excitement is to be avoided if reasonably possible ...."

Today, the average Chinese will take tea — his green tea, at least — for one of two main reasons: To aid digestion and keep his system clean, purging it of toxins. The British and other Western tea-drinkers use it largely for its prime effect — relaxation and the pep it gives to the central nervous system, allaying fatigue. For years, first-aid volunteers have been advised to give strong, sweet tea to anyone suffering from shock — except in cases where they may also be suffering from internal injury. The Observer's Katharine Whitehorn, a confirmed tea-hater, finds this British instinct to reach for the teapot in the middle of a train-crash wreckage and other shocks and disasters a particularly sad comment on the British psyche. "The British insist on believing that a nice cup of tea will cure, or solve, anything. Civil defence is organised so that one person in five will know, not how to dodge bombs or bind wounds, but to put a candle in a flowerpot and heat water for tea. And I saw a boat dangerously adrift in a lake once, with a child fallen into the water, and what was the mother of the child saying? 'Someone put on a kettle for a cup of tea!'"

National idiosyncrasies aside, the British medical profession has obviously done much study on tea, its pharmacology, its effects and its association with health; and this, according to the tea industry, is what the doctors have come up with: a cup of tea

A Canton teashop and *above* tea among funerary offerings for a deceased.

contains, on average, a little under a grain of caffeine. When the infusion is drunk, the caffeine is released gradually. The comforting effect of the warmth of the tea is at once felt, but the stimulus due to the caffeine comes about a quarter of an hour later. Tea is a true stimulant, because of the caffeine it contains, with a long-lasting effect. It allays fatigue and at the same time heightens alertness. It is therefore the ideal reviver on a long car journey (as many long-distance lorry drivers will testify) and in the factory has been shown by research to combat the normal so-called "fatigue curve" by regenerating energy, thus benefiting production.

Data obtained from many sources indicate that the three pharmacologically important constituents of tea are *Caffeine, Theophylline, Theobromine.* The main effect of these is: Caffeine stimulates the central nervous system and respiration; Theophylline has a similar but milder effect and also helps smooth muscle relaxation, diuresis (discharge of urine) and coronary dilation and stimulates the heart; Theobromine acts in much the same way as Theophylline, but to a lesser degree. Considering all the facts, the overall effect of tea drinking is beneficial. Tea also contains *polyphenols,* popularly referred to as *tannin,* the taste of which is allayed by the *casein* in milk. They give tea a bitter taste when it is over-infused and becomes "stewed." This gives rise to the misunderstanding that it "tans the inside of your stomach like leather." There is no evidence of this, and the fact that tea stains the insides of pots and cups has nothing whatsoever to do with this. To avoid misunderstanding, tea chemists usually refer to the polyphenols in tea. This is to distinguish them from "the phenolic materials in tree bark" which are the source of the tannic acid used for tanning leather.

However it is brewed, tea should not be indigestible. Tea is beneficial at all times of the day, but particularly on waking up and after meals. Together with the milk in it, it has a "buffeting" action on the stomach acids which have been collecting during sleep. It takes the heaviness out of a meal by promoting *peristalsis* (getting the intestinal muscles moving). Unless there is medical advice for any reason to the contrary, tea, especially with lemon, which has no calories, is recommended in most diet sheets for slimmers.

That's what the medical profession says, and the military apparently concur. A medical researcher for the United States Air Force has gone on record as suggesting: "Tea is as good an agent for the relief of fatigue as has yet been discovered. In an age when man travels faster, farther, higher and deeper; concocts the biggest bang and the brightest flash of light; produces more material goods; and plays harder then ever conceived possible in the wildest dreams of eras past, it is quite possible that tea-time is what a man needs most to enable him to find respite from his fatigue, anxiety and tension states."

Tea is served on the express train between the Hong Kong border and Canton.

Traditional tea houses have opened up again in the wake of China's Cultural Revolution.

Porcelain sucrier and cover in Japanese Kakiyemon style.

Kakiyemon style imitation — porcelain teapot and cover.

Chinese porcelain with green glaze, c. 1662-1722.

German porcelain with applied and painted decoration, c. 1720.

It is tea-time that has given tea its peculiar and most universal exotica — a phenomenon as diverse as ancient Chinese sipping the "sweetest dew of heaven" with its "gleam like a lake touched by a zephyr" and tweeded matrons discussing their forthcoming church fete or whist drive over rich brown Ceylon blends in Harrods. From the T'ang to Ch'ing dynasties in China, tea drinking as a social ritual was an affectation that only the wealthy, leisured classes could afford. Merchants and the lower workers went to tea-houses in the early mornings and afternoons where they sipped tea and nibbled *dim sum* tidbits, or snacks that could be compared with the Western *hors d'oeuvres*. This tradition of *yum cha*, or tea-lunches, developed and burgeoned in the southern province of Kwangtung, and has

remained popular with the Cantonese, whether those of the People's Republic or those scattered overseas, to this very day. There are still over 100 tea-houses in communist Canton.

Marco Polo described these sort of establishments in detail after his visit to Hangchow in the Yuan dynasty of the late 13th century. Built on a pattern of the large city dwellings of the rich, they had an ornate entrance, a forecourt and a main building behind. Many had adjacent quarters which housed the courtesans, or singsong girls who offered entertainment while the customers drank their tea. The houses vied for prestige custom, boasting luxurious decoration, paintings and framed poems in stylish calligraphy by famous artists, miniature trees, floral decorations, the best porcelain and silver utensils and,

naturally, the finest foods.

But while the Chinese made tea drinking a boisterous social occasion, the Japanese refined it into an art. For them, tea first became the temporal essence of the introverted, mind-exploring ceremonies of Zen — stimulating awareness — then ritualised itself into *Cha-No-Yu*, the Tea Ceremony. First introduced by the priest Eisai and perfected later by the patriarch Sen No Rikyu in the middle 16th century, the tea-house of *Cha-No-Yu* became virtually a shrine and the ceremony itself a rigid paradox (which to Westerners must seem almost excruciating) of relaxation and formality (as excruciating, perhaps, as the Victorian ritual of trying to make breezy small-talk with a teacup and saucer and plate of watercress sandwiches balanced on twitching knees). "Ideally the tea house for *Cha-No-Yu*," writes Robin Moyer, "is an unassuming little hut set away from the main house and surrounded on three sides by a simple garden of rocks and water. The floor is covered with tatami mats around a fire pit. The low roof is thatched with rice straw and the walls are paper shoji supported by thin strips of natural wood. One wall is devoted to an alcove called Tokonoma in which might hang a scroll or painting of calligraphy along with a rock, a spray of flowers or a piece of pottery."[5]

While the water is set to boil in a simple iron pot, its heat-vapours shimmering in the soft sunlight filtering through the paper walls, the formality of the ritual commands tranquillity, purity, respect and harmony on the part of the guests. Perfect balance is maintained in a controlled setting. Politeness pervades: The historian Sir George Sansom described how "guests discuss gravely the merits of some object of art, perhaps one of the utensils they are using, a bowl of which the glaze harbours rich lights ...." In

fact, the Tea Ceremony led to a free-form fashion of Japanese ceramics, called *raku* ware, in which spontaneity of form and glaze is the cardinal rule, and "accident" — the peculiar result of haphazard glaze firings — is its artistry. So, as the Tea Ceremony guests are admiring the mixed hues of a *raku* tea-bowl, the tea-pot gurgles, the boiling water is poured on powdered green tea which is stirred with a bamboo whisk into that treasured "airy froth," and time stops dead in a moment of *satori* — the Infinite Oneness — in which all cares are cast away and only the moment exists.

There are other rules of etiquette as important today as they were in ancient times. Guests are expected to enter the tearoom right foot first, passing through a doorway set so low that a humble entrance is mandatory. Women wear no jewellery, nor do they use perfume; all participants are required to dress simply. They sit with their knees together and drink from a single bowl. The form is to study the bowl first, commenting on its *raku* charm,

then sip slowly before setting it gently to the floor. When they leave, they're expected to go out left foot first.

Plainly there has always been an intense reverence for tea in Japan. A man who was exiled to a remote province wrote to a friend complaining "I have fallen into Hell" — explaining that there was no-one around him capable of conducting the Tea Ceremony, hence no-one with whom he could discuss aesthetic matters. In the 16th century, the originator of *Cha-No-Yu*, Rikyu himself, became so venerated that even Japan's ruler, Hideyoshi, was forced to humble himself before him. Eventually, Hideyoshi decided that Rikyu had become too much of a political threat to his own power and rule — and commanded him to commit *seppuku*, ritual suicide, on the grounds that the tea master had judged certain tea objects incorrectly. And the tea-master, correct in custom and etiquette as he was, naturally complied.

There were certain excesses committed on the fringe of Japan's tea ritual — Hideyoshi

Tea houses in Canton.

staged the grandest and possibly most vulgar tea party ever given, the Kitano Tea Party, which lasted 10 days and which thousands upon thousands of Japanese attended, bringing their own kettles and tatami mats; and a wealthy Japanese tea addict made a pilgrimage to Tibet, there to stage another huge tea drinking bash in which no less than 4,000 Buddhist lamas, seated in rows, each received two bowls of tea from the pilgrim's own hands. But generally, the ultra-refined simplicity of *Cha-No-Yu* has reigned supreme in Japanese society, and its Zen fundamentals have long underscored Japan's art and culture. "Architects, gardeners, designers and craftsmen of all kinds work in concert with the *Chajin* (Men of Tea) so that their vision has been passed on to the most everyday objects — textiles, baskets, kitchen implements, common teapots, even televisions and hundreds of other objects in which the Japanese show their good taste to best advantage."[6]

The Chinese were not far behind the Japanese, however, when it came to blending tea with art. In Lu Yu's time, any tea drinker of repute and self-esteem would insist on taking his tea only from the finest, icy-blue porcelain cups made in Yueh Chow — the delicate tone of the cup's glaze enhancing the tone of the tea. During the later Ming dynasty renaissance of Chinese ceramics and all other forms of art, blue and white "Mingware" from Ching-te Chen was the fashionable tea drinking receptacle. Teapots were also being refined. The Ming period saw the rise to prominence of the Yi Hsing teapot of unglazed biscuit- to dark brown-coloured fired clays taken from a Kiangsi province area about 150 miles west of Shanghai. The Yi Hsing teapots were first moulded into a multitude of shapes ranging from a simple squat, fat-bellied yet sleek and streamlined form to highly stylised creations in the shape of fruit, flowers, vegetables and even musical instruments. The blended colours of the clay gave them their distinctive appeal; no

Part of English (Caughley) porcelain toy tea service 1772-99.

French soft-paste porcelain with enamel colours, mid-18th century.

Teaport and creamer, British, c. 1800.

glazing was applied either outside or within. But then, late in the Ming dynasty and in the following Ch'ing period, subtlety and natural style gave way to ostentation and a craze for glaze — with the added *kitsch* of famille rose enamelling — and the original Yi Hsing style disappeared. Today, antique Yi Hsing teapots are worth a fortune. If you can find them.

The development of the Chinese tea-ware is important not only for its cultural value but for the influence it had, along with the tea itself, on the British and Europeans. Japan's Tea Ceremony and its *raku* pottery may have been culturally superior to what China had to offer, but Japan closed its doors on the West, withdrew into its own mysticism, while the luxuries and traditional products of China's culture flooded the Western world. Yi Hsing teapots and the blue and white Ming tea-ware were introduced to Britain in support of tea — *literally* supporting the stuff in the ship's holds. "In East Indiamen days the main aim of stowage was to keep the tea reasonably dry and sweet through the long steamy voyage while the stinking bilge slopped to and fro. It was done by the remarkable custom of putting not tea but China in the lowest tier; this accounts for the immense quantities of utility blue-and-white which figured in the (East India) Company's auctions and which stock our antique shops to this day. Above the china came the cheapest grades of Bohea, and so on until one arrived at the fine Hysons and Gunpowders, stowed well above the water-line, with very often a top dressing of silk."[7]

Yi Hsing earthenware was imitated all over Europe. So was the delicate Chinese porcelain, which the British, Germans and Dutch copied as "bone china." Josiah Wedgwood refined the Yi Hsing-inspired earthenwares into "creamwares," then went on to produce "stonewares, usually unglazed and hard enough to be polished on the lathe." Meanwhile, the huge demand for teapots — and then teacups when the British found they needed something to drink the tea from

— led to the rise of the ornately styled, sometimes grotesque Staffordshire ceramics. By and large, the British weren't successful with their ceramic teapots. Artist potters found that when they had to "fiddle with the spout, handle and lid of a single teapot (they were) apt to come up with something lumpy and impractical, which drips." On the commercial side, Britain has continued to import much of its ceramic tea-ware from China and Japan.

The British did much better with their own teacraft innovation — silverware. Their silversmiths started with teapots and then went on to develop the complete range of tea-ware, including teapot, sugar bowl and milk jug, tea kettle (superseded by the tea urn), teaspoons, tea-strainers, sugar tongs and large trays to carry the whole paraphernalia. "The earliest identifiable English silver teapots date from about 1690," says Denys Forrest, "but they quickly took their place among the most popular and enjoyable specimens of the silversmith's art. The small pear-shaped pots of 1710-20 (some of which, alas, had little lamps beneath them to keep the tea stewing) are perfect evocations of the age of good manners." Silver tea-ware reached its peak in the "grand extravagances" of the Regency period (1800-1830) when "the teapot was frequently of a compressed shape on four cast paw feet or, in simpler versions, on ball feet. Gadrooned edges and half-fluting up the bodies became general, and the spout was usually fairly short and curved. One or two pots were highly decorated. As early as 1803 Digby Scott and Benjamin Smith made an elaborately chased pot with the spout rising to the form of a grouse's head ... During the 1820s the melon-shape became firmly established, the panels richly chased with scrollwork, flowers and foliage in imitation of the Rococo."[8]

The tea caddy, or canister, derived from the Chinese term *catty* — a measurement of weight equivalent to 0.6 kg — was also very much in vogue in these times. At first they were

porcelain jars, or in some cases glass containers. A glass caddy of the early 19th century, 18 inches high and "shaped like a huge brandy glass (with a) delicate glass lid," is on show these days in the Hampshire offices of Twinings. "Tea was expensive in those days," says the company, "and some people kept their precious few ounces in a widemouthed bottle with a glass stopper, like a large scent bottle. For those who liked to blend their own tea there were tea caddies on tea chests with a glass mixing bowl which lay between the two separate storage sections, one for black and one for green tea. The chests were often made of satinwood decorated with Chinese figures. Sometimes they were called tea boxes. A more elaborate version took the form of a table, also known as a teapoy, of which the top slid aside to reveal a mixing bowl and four storage compartments. One of these was presented to Princess Elizabeth in the days before she became Queen."

Caddies came in all shapes, sizes and materials. There were caddies made of tortoiseshell, mother-of-pearl, ivory, lacquer and papier mache and wood "in all possible permutations of inlay and veneer." But again, Britain's silversmiths gave the caddy its special place in dynastic art — a magnificent example being a fluted tea caddy with bright-cut borders designed and crafted by John Robins in 1796, a collector's item which can be seen in Judith Banister's *Late Georgian and Regency Silver*. So highly prized are these silver caddies today, that Britain's Garrard and Company Ltd, the Crown Jewellers, were commissioned in the early 1970s to reproduce for a Canadian client an 18th-century sterling silver tea caddy exhibited in the Victoria and Albert Museum. "It was a remarkable request," says Garrards, "as nothing of this nature had been attempted within the last 20 years, owing to the skilled workmanship and high standard of engraving that is required to reproduce such works of art." The client was so pleased with the result that he commissioned Garrards to

Porcelain teapot painted by William Billingslay of Mansfield, Staffs., c. 1800; Porcelain tinted with enamel, English (Derby), c.1750, Silver teapot by N. Odiot, Paris,1819-38.

White porcelain teacup and saucer with pierced design, French (Sevres) 1866-76,

Porcelain, painted with enamel and gilt, English, probably 18th century.

reproduce another silver caddy as a present for his wife. According to the company, the cost of reproducing both pieces was more than £1,000 each, probably more than the cost of the originals.

The exotica of tea, in this respect, is its artistic legacy — fine, highly priced antique china and silverware that have joined the lists of precious items sought at the auctions of Sotheby's and Christies; or the large and constant turnover of less expensive imitations and oddities that draw crowds of British, Americans and Europeans each weekend to London's Portobello Road.

The oldest, best and most valued antique tea-ware is almost impossible to find on the open market nowadays; most of it is safely tucked away in private collections. But Twinings came across a celebrated piece quite by accident during the renovation of the London warehouse of one of its subsidiaries — and it turned out to be nothing less than perhaps the biggest teapot in the world, an ornate ceramic giant measuring 2ft 6ins high, over 6 feet in girth and capable of

serving no less than 13½ gallons of tea. Chinese scenes of the growing, picking, fermenting and shipping of tea are painted in a colourful pageant around the pot's huge bowl. Twinings say the exact origins of the teapot are unknown, but it's believed to have been made for display at the first of the great international exhibitions held in Hyde Park between May and October 1851.

"However, it has been established that the teapot was acquired, probably immediately after the Crystal Palace Exhibition of 1851, by Calverts, a Nottingham firm of tea and coffee blenders with a long tradition in the business. There is in existence a press cutting which not only illustrates the teapot as one of Calverts' treasures, but claims tea from it was poured for Prince Albert and Queen Victoria at the Great Exhibition." The giant Teapot is now a Twinings promotional treasure, put on show at international fairs and trade exhibitions to remind the world that there is far more to the exotica of tea than tea itself.

Compared with the exquisite grace of their traditional *Cha-No-*

Yu, the Japanese would undoubtedly regard tea-time in Britain as a tasteless, almost barbaric affair. And it probably is, if you consider that outside the genteel afternoon ritual of the upper middle-class drawing room, much British tea-drinking is done amid the clamour and smoky, grease-laden atmosphere of cafes and quick-serve eating houses or a percussion of cash-register bells and bargain announcements in department stores. The twain of East and West have still not met so far as tea drinking is concerned. While the Chinese and Japanese still *celebrate* their tea, the British *consume* it, and in such regular quantities that even that devil's advocate of the tea trade, Katharine Whitehorn, can be forgiven her fulminations against tea when encountering this sort of daily tea ritual:

"Every time I have my mother or my mother-in-law to stay it is the same. They need a cup of tea to wake them up. They have a cup of tea with breakfast. Just as you've got over that, they have something in the middle of the morning — tea, perhaps, after lunch, at tea-time, and even (since my mother comes from Scotland) at 10 in the evening another cup is required. You send up a cry of joy when your last baby is finally off two-hourly feeds and on to proper meals, and then your elder relations on their two-hourly schedule come to stay and you're back where you started.

"My mother favours China tea, because her father (a Presbyterian minister) once helped a widow's son to get a job in a tea company, and he sent her a great chest of the stuff from the Far East every Christmas. My mother-in-law, on the other hand, likes raw strong Indian, the kind in which you can stand the spoon up, which revolts me. My mother-in-law thinks tea-bags are sluttish; I think the stuff's so nasty anyway you might at least let yourself off the horrible business of getting the leaves out of the pot."

The grace and gentility of British tea drinking peaked in the Regency era, when the afternoon ritual involved fine silver and china and "since in every house, large or small, drinking tea was so important a social occasion, those who could purchased a large tea tray on which to assemble the tea service and the china needed for the ceremony."[9] Otherwise, apart from the brown gruel and thick white mugs (or plastic disposable beakers) of today's lunch counters, British "teas" have probably most been associated with young Victorian men strangling in starched collars, balancing cups and plates on their trembling knees while the lady of the house nods appreciatively on the *chaise longue* and her marriageable daughter thumps out songs about birds in gilded cages on the piano. But the history of the development of the British "tea ceremony" is no less exotic for this; indeed, it's extremely fascinating.

Tea was first served in the coffee houses that spread through inner London, the area now known as the West End, in the early 1700s, one of the first of which was Tom's Coffee House at Devereux Court, birthplace of Twinings. Gentry, intelligentsia and merchants frequented these establishments, discussing

politics, transacting business or simply sporting themselves over tea, coffee chocolate, brandy or the Turkish aniseed-based *arak*. If Daniel Defoe's account of his daily rounds of the coffee houses in 1714 is typical of the times, then those times were such that tea and coffee drinkers never had it so good.

"If you would know of our manner of living, 'tis thus: We rise by Nine, and those that frequent men's levees find entertainment at them till eleven, or, as in Holland go to tea tables. About twelve the beau monde assemble in several coffee or chocolate houses; the best of which are the Cocoa Tree and White's Chocolate houses, St James's, The Smyrna, Mrs Rochford's and the British coffee-houses; and all these so near to one another that in less than an hour you see the company of them all. We are carried to these places in chairs (or Sedans) which here are very cheap, a guinea a week or a shilling per hour, and your chairmen serve you for porters to run on errands, as your gondoliers do at Venice.

"If it be fine weather, we take a turn into the Park till two, when we go to dinner; and if it be dirty, you are entertained at picquet or basset at White's, or you may go and talk politics at the Smyrna or St James's. At two we generally go to dinner; ordinaries (public, fixed-price meals in inns) are not so common here as abroad, yet the French have set up two or three good ones for the convenience of foreigners in Suffolk Street, where one is tolerably well served, but the general way here is to make a party at the coffee house to go to dine at the tavern, where we sit till six, when we go to the play; except you are invited to the table of some great man which strangers are always courted to and nobly entertained."

What a life! The ladies enjoyed it too, as Arthur Reade recalled in his *Tea and Tea Drinking* (1884): "In Queen Anne's reign ladies of fashion used to flock to Messrs Twining's house in Devereux Court in order to sip the enlivening brew (of tea) in their small china cups, much as nowadays they sit in their

carriages eating ices at the door of Gunter's in Berkeley Square on hot days." The idyllic rounds of the coffee houses ended, however, when the political discussions of the menfolk became too impassioned, and too threatening for the Establishment to tolerate, and Queen Anne and her Dukes and Duchesses launched tea drinking on its gradual but inexorable path to democratization by making it a fashionable social thing to do at court. A century later, the Duchess of Bedford hastened the whole process into the private home by introducing Britain's answer to *Cha-No-Yu* — the afternoon tea. And the afternoon tea provided the setting for that great revolution in British tea drinking — the switch from Chinese to Indian blends. Once weaned away from them, the British just wouldn't accept the traditional delicacy of straight China teas any more. As Sir Edmund Hornby grouched in 1865: "After dinner we were served again with Tea — that is with a few leaves of tea served in an egg cup with a little hot water poured over them. It was not an exhilarating beverage but far better in its simple honesty than champagne. This is the usual way tea is made in China, and a more wishy-washy mixture is not easy to conceive. Indeed, it is a rather remarkable fact that it is very difficult to get a good cup of tea in China — whether it is the water or the milk or the sugar that renders it so palatable in England, I know not, but somehow or other tea in China does not taste like tea at home."

Tastes changed to the hearty Assam and Ceylon teas, with milk and sugar, and tea-drinking fashions, as they became more popular and public, evolved from the 18th century "tea gardens" of London — like Ranelagh Gardens, Chelsea, which featured a huge Rotunda and "smart little suppers served in the arbours or in 'boxes' under cover" — to "tea pavilions" that became a feature of the huge 19th century international exhibitions — like the "Bishop's Palace Tea Rooms" at the Glasgow international show of 1888, "with waitresses dressed in Mary

Stuart costumes. Backroom tea sessions served for the select clientele of some big business houses led in turn to the spread of tea-shops, the most famous of which have been the chain of Lyons Tea Shops. The first Lyons establishment opened at 213 Piccadilly and offered a setting for tea-sipping ladies and gents in which "the white and gold fascia was much the same as now, but red silk covered the walls and gas-lighted chandeliers hung from the ceiling. You sat in a red plush chair and were served by a very smart waitress in a grey uniform with voluminous skirts down to the floor."

On the supply side, the democratization of Britain's tea is vividly exemplified by the rags-to-riches story of one of today's tea-retailing giants, Tesco. Denys Forrest recounts how in *Pile it high, Sell it Cheap*[10] Mr Maurice Corina tells the riveting tale of how 2nd Class Air Mechanic Jack Cohen, son of an East End tailor called Avroam Kohen, came out of the RAF in March 1919 with a £30 gratuity and no job. He hated the idea of drawing the dole, and invested his £30 in returned NAAFI canned goods. Piling these onto a barrow, he went out into the street markets of Hackney. His other assets were a loud voice, a quick wit and a genius for mental arithmetic. Somehow he made his way, but it was after coming a cropper with soap that he had his first real break. He met Mr T.E. Stockwell, of the small Tower Hill firm of Torring & Stockwell, who had a few chests of blended tea on offer. Jack did a deal at 9d per lb and had the tea put up in ½lb packets to sell at 6d a time. He needed something to go on the label, and from the names of his suppliers and himself was evolved the word TESCO. The 6d packets went well among the East Enders. Soon Jack was ordering in 50 chest lots, wholesaling came next, then a few stalls or shops with roll-down fronts, and there followed the explosive story of Tesco's rise to a business with a £250-million turnover, and a knighthood for its ebullient head."

In World War II, tea and the factory canteens took their place

Italian porcelain teapot with moulded and enamelled decoration, Vezzi factory, Venice, c. 1725.

on a large scale in British industry, largely through the efforts of the YMCA and Empire Tea Bureau which launched the syndrome by first providing what were called "Tea Cars" for the British fighting man. As the bureau's commissioner, R.L. Barnes, described it: "Our recipe was: Take one or two multipots (big tea urns) from a holiday camp trolley and place on a repainted secondhand van; add mugs, milk, sugar, chocolate, biscuits, cake, razor blades, postage stamps etc., mix well together. Result — one mobile canteen or Tea Car." By the end of 1940 the YMCA had 40 Tea Cars bringing hot cuppas and a bit of cheer to the troops. Twenty-four took their teas all the way to France, where their drivers and assistants got caught in the disastrous Dunkirk and Boulogne evacuations, and only just made it back to England in one piece.

As for Katharine Whitehorn's "sluttish" tea-bags, any self-respecting tea drinker would consider the least said about them the better. The Americans took to them first with that inherent ingenuity that promotes and celebrates all innovative and especially labour-saving devices;

and it wasn't until the 1950s that the tea-bag crossed the Atlantic and began flooding the British market. But when it did, the tea-bag ironically came to the aid of the British tea industry at a time when it sorely needed help. Instant coffee had hit the British scene, and had become increasingly popular with young couples — so much so that it all but halted the growth of the tea industry. It is only in the last decade that tea has begun to forge ahead again as the leader in household beverages in Britain, and the tea-bag has been largely responsible for this upsurge. It's estimated that by 1980, tea-bags will command 50 percent of the British tea retail market. But tea-bags, for all the prejudice that still gnashes around them, are, even now, part of the history of tea. At a Bureau of Standards seminar held in Colombo, Sri Lanka in 1978, it became known that not only is "instant tea" becoming established on many of the world's tea tables, but even newer forms of tea and tea-based products have already been developed, including "tea cider, tea wine, carbonated tea and, (one hesitates to mention it), *tea pills!*"

English, mid-18th century porcelain and enamel cream jug.

Queen Anne silver teapot, London hallmark, 1719.

But even the prospect of tea pills tends to pale against a wider, truly exotic background of strange, sometimes sinister concoctions that have, through the centuries, laid claim to the title *tea*. They are, indeed, teas — in that they are infused from vegetable matter and drunk as a medicine or stimulant. But they certainly have nothing to do with *Camellia sinensis* — just as the purple tea introduced to Vancouver by a man named Jervis in the 1950s came, in fact, from his lilac hedge, and the imitation Chinese tea invented by a Frenchman came from birch-leaves scented with Florence iris.

Aside from the counterfeits, just as there are around 1,500 blends and types of orthodox tea, so are there hundreds, perhaps thousands of teas made from the leaves, roots, seeds and berries of herbs and a great many different shrubs and plants. The Javanese make tea from the roasted leaves of tea's direct rival, coffee. The Malays make it from a species of the myrtle tree. The Mauritians use orchids. The Texas Indians of the United States used to get high as kites drinking "Carolina tea" or *cassena* brewed from a holly tree. A pale green tea made from raspberry leaves has been used as a tonic by pregnant women for centuries — it relaxes the muscles of the pelvic region and uterus and helps stop diaorrhea. The berries of wild rose bushes have long been brewed as a tonic and protection against colds — they're literally loaded with vitamin C. Ginseng tea, a major product today of Korea, has been known to the Chinese for over

two thousand years as a stimulant and disease-resisting tonic. Westerners have just as long been sceptical about ginseng's extravagant claims, but the latest research into the root by United States chemists has shown that it does, in fact, promote strength and resistance against sickness. Korea's world-wide ginseng marketing has become so sophisticated that the extract is put out in boxes of gold-foil packets. The taste is awful, despite what the information on the products of the Il Hwa Ginseng Tea Company of Seoul, says. "Il Hwa Ginseng Tea is made by extracting the major constituents of Korean ginseng roots, special products of Korea, using a highly concentrated alcohol at a low temperature and pressure. This most pure extract is then mixed with dextrose anhydrous and dried at a low temperature to make the best Korean ginseng tea products, having a most flavourful taste just like the fresh roots themselves (no chemicals added). Mix the contents of one tea packet to a cup of hot or cold water. Add sugar or honey to taste and stir well." Sugar or honey is essential, for most Western palates would associate the flavourful taste of the fresh ginseng roots with the soles of the shoes of the man who dug it up.

As for other unorthodox teas, all guaranteed to lift the senses or sometimes blow them to the four winds, there are four that have established themselves in the dictionary: "*Abyssinian tea* is a narcotic, exhilarating tea from the leaves of the kat shrub

cultivated by the Arabs. Bitter, it is usually sweetened with honey. Chewing the fresh leaves is intoxicating. *Labrador tea* is made from an evergreen shrub of North America. Its narcotic, soothing and stimulating brew comforted early hunters, trappers, miners and explorers in the North. It lends its headiness to Scandinavian beer. *Oswego tea* is brewed from fragrant mint that sports a head of bright flowers. The (American) Indians regarded it as a medicine. The Shakers who settled in Oswego, New York, gave it its name. They considered it a tonic. *Hamburger tea* is not what you expect. It is a laxative made from senna leaves, manna, coriander and tartaric acid."[11]

Though the British had been taking herbal infusions like camomile, sage, catnip, sarsaparilla and dock for ages, largely as folk medicines, they didn't take too kindly to the first attempts to blend herbs into their precious tea market in the 19th century. When a retailer named Snelling tried to market

Teapot and cream jug, porcelain moulded in relief and painted, English (Chelsea) 1745-50.

German tin-glazed earthenware, (Hochst) c. 1750.

Black basalt ware teapot of early 19th century.

Chinese red stoneware with moulded relief, early 18th century.

teas blended with hops in the 1870s, the tea Establishment got it swept off the shelves, "presumably as a hideous case of adulteration." Earlier, another enterprising merchant had tried to introduce Britons to a widely-enjoyed South African herbal tea which, in fact, has the taste of China green tea and is exported to South Africans living abroad. This venture, too, had about as much success as a lead balloon. "It was on December 21, 1867, that Mr George Townend of Townend Brothers rashly offered a parcel of 'bush tea' from Natal. This herb product ... consumed under the name Rooibos, has in fact nothing to do with *Camellia sinensis*. The appearance of two samples on the 'ink table' in the middle of the room was greeted with yells of protest. Mr Holborn suggested that they should be taken away to the drug department and although, in spite of the uproar, the unfortunate broker refused to abandon the sale, there were no bids and what the *Grocer* called 'a monstrous bale of

rubbish' was withdrawn."[12]

Today, herbal teas are enjoying a wide commercial revival in Britain, Europe and most especially the United States, where, for example, Twinings are driving into the vast beverage market with a new range of blended herbal tea-bags. Launched at America's annual Fancy Food Fair in Chicago, the herbal teas got an initial thumbs-up from Mimi Sheraton, a writer for the prestigious *New York* magazine. "Twinings new herb tea bags were good, as herb teas go," she stated, "and though I do not favour such brews, these seemed stronger and more fragrant than the brands usually found in Health Food stores. The rose hip tea was ruby-red and sour but bracing, the camomile was soothing and smelled of sunshine and the verbene had a light lemony perfume. Linden and mint were less interesting, unless of course you like linden and mint."

Another important herbal tea market is West Germany, where herb blends account for a staggering 60 percent of the country's total tea consumption. Belgium and Italy are also testing their palates on camomiles, rose hips and lindens, and in Canada, where they drink about 2½ lbs of orthodox tea per head a year, "skyrocketing prices, combined with concern about the adverse effects of caffeine and tannic acid on the nervous and digestive systems, have driven many people to search for alternative drinks." The Canadians are taking a fresh look at around 25 herbal concoctions for a start, ranging

from cedar teas that are said to have saved Jacques Cartier's expedition from dying of scurvy when the French discovered Canada, to "the more exotic (wild raspberry and sassafras) to the downright daunting (stinging nettles)."[13]

But it is the coffee-laden United States market that attracts the big orthodox tea and herbal tea suppliers of today. As already mentioned, the US has long been an important consumer of Japanese and Taiwanese green teas and oolongs, and, with coffee prices going slowly through the roof, it has lately earned second placing on the list of countries importing the stronger Indian tea blends. With the powerful Food and Drug Administration currently coming up almost day after day with alarming findings on the effects of chemical medicines and food additives, with the caffeine content of coffee already so widely feared that coffee manufacturers are marketing de-caffeinated brands, more and more herbal teas are moving from the specialist health food stores to the common supermarket shelves. And more and more Americans are "learning to relieve their sore throats with gargles of slippery-elm tea, their headaches with comfrey root, cold or flu by drinking pots of spicy yarrow and sage tea.

"One reason for the rediscovery of herbal teas, drunk at one time or other by every culture in the world, is the cancer scare. 'We're learning that chemical pollution of food and the environment may contribute to cancer, and this has been one of the factors responsible for a return to more natural therapies,' says Dr Robert Giller, a New York general practitioner. 'Rather than loading up on synthetic chemicals for minor aches and pains, people are giving a second look at age-old remedies.'"[14]

The range of herb teas, or *tisanes* as they are termed in their infused form, is almost as long as a botanical dictionary, but the most common ingredients can be listed as camomile, sage, ginger, peppermint, valerian (doesn't that name ring a bell?), heather flowers, maize silk, cherry stalks, bearberry leaves, rose berries, cinnamon, allspice, anise (aniseed), barley, carob, lemon grass and lemon verbena, spearmint, comfrey, eucalyptus, hibiscus, blackberry leaves, hops, basil, dandelion, rosemary, thyme, licorice, juniper, celery, fennel .... Then there's that exotic South American mate, or matte, known as Paraguayan tea, whose leaves are rich in caffeine and is a highly stimulating drink produced cheaply and drunk in considerable amounts in Peru, Chile, Argentina, Brazil, Bolivia and Paraguay. The dried, powdered leaves are placed in hollowed-out gourds, boiling water is poured in and the gourds are sealed with tops. The drinkers then take turns to sip the infusion through special straws known as *bombillas*. Mate may be drunk hot or cold and with or without sugar, lemon juice or rum kirsch. Needless to say, in its elementary form it tends to make South American life look a lot brighter.

Herbal infusions can also be taken as beauty treatments, either drunk or applied to the face and body as rubs, masks shampoos, skin-cleansers, baths — doing wonders for the hair, teeth, nails, skin, eyes and that most dreaded of young people's problems, acne. In her attractive and definitive book *Feed Your Face* — a complete herbal guide to natural beauty and health — Dian Buchman explains that you prepare an infusion of herbal ingredients just as you would brew strong tea. "Unless you want it to be stronger, the basic recipe is a pint of boiling water to two tablespoons of leaves or flowers. It is important to remember that leaves and flowers must *never be boiled*. You pour the boiling water *over* the herb, and you let it steep. Unlike tea or coffee, which take only a few minutes, a herb should be steeped far longer. The minimum time for cosmetic use (it takes longer for medicinal

Unglazed stoneware (jasper ware) from factory of Josiah Wedgewood, 1775-85.

use) is 15 minutes, but the longer you allow the herb to steep the more valuable it becomes. Three hours is the maximum time needed to extract the properties fully. *Always keep the pot covered* during steeping. After steeping, the herbs will fall to the bottom of the pot; so you can either skim off the water, which is now infused with herb principles, or strain it into a jug."

Apart from outward beauty, Ms Buchman has some good suggestions on the sort of herbs best suited to beauty sleep, or, more significantly, that 20th century phenomenon, insomnia. Peppermint, camomile, aromatic woodruff, sage and wild lettuce teas are good sedatives or sleep inducers or prolongers, she says, while the early American settlers used both red bergamot tea (bergamot is an ingredient of Earl Grey) and pennyroyal for relaxed slumber. She quotes the Swiss priest-herbalist, Father Kunzle as offering two suggestions for "harmless sleeping potions. He recommends 4 parts of golden rod to one part juniper, or a calming tea of lady's mantle and cowslips combined. Cowslips have been used for centuries in England for nightly tea. The American herbalist Jethro Kloss advises a warm bath and hot tea for immediate sleep, and he suggests any of the following herbs steeped in boiling water for 20 minutes: lady's slipper, valerian, catnip, skullcap or hops, especially hops. He says that these herbs will not only induce sleep but will tone up the stomach and nerves, and never leave any bad after-effect."[15]

The Japanese, Chinese and even the Arabs have studded their little gems of exotica to the fringes of orthodox tea, either with herb blends, additives and unusual or even bizarre uses of tea. *Mu* tea, an infusion of ginseng and no less than 15 medicinal herbs, is enjoyed by both the Chinese and Japanese, while the Japanese have specialities like lotus tea, *kohren* tea made from raw ginger, roasted barley tea, and *bancha* — everyday green tea with a dash of *tamari*, a pure soybean concentrate, which is said to give a "bracing lift" in the event of fatigue. The Chinese have their almond tea — ground almonds simply infused in water — plum and quince tea which is served after Mongolian Barbecue and ginger tea which is taken after the seasonal delicacy, Shanghai hairy crab.

The Japanese use tea-bags as eye-pads as a beauty treatment

Hard-paste porcelain decorated with enamel colours, Swiss (Zurich), c. 1770.

to refresh the eyes. They use dried, used tea leaves to stuff pillows and pin-cushions; and they clean their tatami mats with tea — they say it gives them a fresh smell. In the Middle East, bedouin women use tea with henna for dyeing their hair. Chinese ivory carvers have long been using black tea to stain and provide colouring for certain features of their artwork; and in Hong Kong and Singapore, tea is often used today to stain modern carvings and give them an "antique" look.

Even the British have found some unusual uses for tea outside the teapot. They know that tea rubbed on badly sunburned skin relieves the pain. And in World War II, strong tea was used as an improvised cosmetic, giving colour to the skin when beauty creams, lotions and powders — like nylon stockings — were right down the bottom of the list of production priorities.

By and large, the British are a pretty conservative lot when it comes to the exotica of tea. They *love* it and, indeed, are addicted to it, but as they themselves would say, that's that! Though herbal teas have been an essential part of their folklore, and are taken occasionally by country folk today, there's no sign as yet of anything like a national rush to experiment with Twinings' rose hips or camomile, or the American Celestial Seasonings' *Morning Thunder, Lemon Mist* or *Matte Orange Spice*. But the British have, in their own way, added mystique to the story of tea. For one thing, they adopted an ancient Chinese custom of searching the insides of bells, and upturned teacups, for auspicious or ominous signs and developed it into a passion for fortune-telling, or tea-leaf reading. By taking a cup with a small amount of liquor and dregs in it, swirling it around and then slowly turning it upside down — so that the liquor drains off and the leaves stay stuck to the bottom of the bowl — they can peer into the haphazard formations and patterns of the leaves and interpret symbols ranging in fortune from happiness and wealth to absolute ruin; like a *circle*, a favourable

Silver gilt tea caddy in the style of Gribelin, English, c. 1700.

Silver tea caddy, London, 1766.

ea kettle and stand, Charles Kandler, London, 1727-37.

ch silver gilt sugar bowl, J.B.C. Odiot, 1809-19.

Tea urn, silver gilt, J.B.C. Odiot, 1798-1809.

Porcelain teapot, French (Sèvres), 1814.

sign meaning that all projects will be successfully concluded; a *bouquet* — the blessing of staunch friends, prosperity and success, and for the lover a happy marriage; a *bottle* — a warning that all excesses must be avoided; a *cart* can have a double meaning — to a person of high status it can mean decline, or it can denote gain through a sudden business transaction or a legacy; a *coffin* — enough said, though it does not necessarily mean death, perhaps only illness brought on through carelessness, neglect or excess.[16]

"In the Scottish highlands," the Schapiras write, "the tea-leaf reader was known as the 'spae-wife.' She read her own tea leaves every morning from her breakfast cup, and those of her friends who came to visit during the day. She looked not into the far future, but only into the twenty-four hours to come. She would predict such things as the weather, if a letter would come and from whom, whether it was a good day to take the stock to market, whether a sick person would recover. An anonymous Highland seer, author of *Tea-Cup Reading and the Art of Fortune-Telling by Tea-Leaves*, claimed that 'many of the minor happenings of life could be foreseen with considerable accuracy' but that those who charged for the service and claimed to be able to predict the future were simply exploiting their gullible clients."[17]

Another bizarre aspect of the exotica of tea, kept alive even into these times by the British and their Anglo-Saxon colleagues around the world, is the constantly-raging debate on how the perfect cup of tea should be made — how much tea should go into the pot, whether the milk should be added to the tea or vice versa. The debate is nothing new — it's been going on for centuries and its various conflicting dogmas have depended on where in the world it's drunk and how, in fact, its drinkers prefer to drink it. Some people drink tea plain. Others like to add milk and sugar or lemon slices or juice. A few like to kick their brews along with a dash of rum, scotch or cognac. In Tibet a cup of tea is served with a lump of yak butter

Porcelain kettle and burner, painted in enamels, French, late 18th century.

111

Silver teapot with stand and burner, London (Simon Pantin) 1705-6.

floating on its surface. The Tibetans are so fond of this that they drink at least 10 or 20 cups of the yakky stuff a day. Chinese connoisseurs would no more add milk, sugar or lemon to tea than they would ferment milk and make cheese. For them, nothing must spoil the rich natural fragrance and flavour of tea, and it must be drunk with relish. Not swallowed in a gulp in the English way to quench a thirst, warm up a chilled body or to calm frayed nerves, but sipped and savoured as one would a good cognac. It should be drunk from small fine porcelain cups, each mouthful swilled slowly around the tongue, held a moment to enjoy it to its fullest, then swallowed slowly.

Taiwan's leading producer of oolong teas has his own traditional tea-brewing formula: "The tea reaches its best at the instant when one opens the teapot, after the tea has steeped for three to five minutes. The quality of water, teapot and teacup all contribute to the making of good tea. Pure mountain springs supply the best quality water for tea. Teapot and cups made of clay or Chinese porcelain of high quality will be better than ordinary glass cups."

According to one Hong Kong connoisseur "the colour of the infusion is in inverse value to its quality. Good teas do not need fermentation, do not improve with the darkness of colour usually favoured by tea drinkers of the West." One of Hong Kong's oldest tea merchants considers that most tea leaves should be at least a few years old before they're drunk. But all that doesn't offer much in the way of help to the British, Americans, Canadians, Australians, New Zealanders and other major contemporary tea consumers, most of whom have neither the benefit of pure mountain waters, nor high quality porcelain nor antique teas with which to seek perfection. To them, the great tea-making debate comes down to its purest fundamentals.

"Britain has its champions of the meticulous in making tea," Tom Lambert, a staff writer of the *Los Angeles Times* observed with a certain bewilderment in 1973. These were "men or women who will argue doggedly that the teapot should or should not be warmed before the tea is made, that milk should or should not be poured into a cup before it is filled with brew from the pot. Now comes the British Standards

Silver gilt tea service with enamel decoration made by Gueyton, Paris, 1862.

Institute, an independent organisation financed with government and industry grants and private contributions, which helps establish standards for consumer goods, with a draft proposal on how to make a good 'cuppa.' In its recipe, designed 'to provide a common approach to their job by professional tea-tasters who are involved in the demanding task of selecting and blending teas,' the BSI 'recommends the design of the appropriate pot, the type of water which is suitable, the time of infusion, the order in which the milk is best added, and other relevant factors'."

But rather than establishing a common standard, the BSI only made matters worse. For one thing, it advised tea brewers to put in tea "with a weight of two percent of the mass of water," and to fill the pot to within "four millimetres of the brim." It said nothing about warming the pot first, and on the subject of milk applied what might be called a popular bureaucratic ploy — recommending neither one thing nor the other, but covering itself on both counts. "Unless it is

Silver teapot presented by George Berkeley to the East India Company, 1670.

contrary to normal practice, said the Institute ... pour milk into the cup first. But if you like to add milk afterwards 'experience has shown that best results are obtained if the temperature of the tea is in the range of 65° to 80°C when milk is added'.[18]

Quite naturally, the Institute's recommendations were received with a howl of indignation and derision. People questioned whether the Institute was referring to tea or a laboratory experiment, what with its millimetres and two percent of the mass of water. Others insisted that the Institute had ignored the most important step in tea-brewing — warming the pot first. The Canadians got in on the act, with the Canadian Tea Council issuing its own recommended rules on making tea, and a tea connoisseur in Vancouver pointing out that the "brewing time depends entirely upon the tea. Darjeeling may take seven or eight minutes. A Ceylon, only three or four. A China tea can be served almost immediately." Then the American Board of Tea Experts put out their own version of the easy step-by-step guide to making tea. It began: "Use a tea pot. It holds temperatures at a very high level. Don't steep tea in a cup. It lets the best flavours and aromas escape." This remarkable observation presumably had something to do with the American *penchant* for tea-bags.

To be absolutely candid, the correct way to make tea is, as Jacksons of Piccadilly advise, *the way you prefer it*. But there are basic guidelines put out by the major tea companies and producers that will give even the most novice tea-maker a good cuppa, even if the rules do continue to get confused and differ slightly here and there. This is the Twinings guide to the best method of making tea:

1. Use good tea, preferably a speciality tea. One and a half teaspoons for each person and one for the pot. But be guided by the recommendations on the packet. Always keep the tea in an airtight container.

2. Use fresh cold water to fill the kettle and then bring to the boil.

3. As soon as the kettle boils turn it off.

4. Heat the teapot — preferably a China teapot. Metal teapots sometimes affect the taste of some of the more subtle teas.

5. Take the teapot to the boiling water.

6. Brew for three or five minutes, stirring before pouring.

7. Cold fresh milk should be poured into the cup before the tea — this way it mixes better with the tea. With some speciality teas it is better to drink them without milk if the full character of the tea is to be enjoyed. And if tea is taken with lemon it is better not to squeeze it, as it will usually blunt the true taste of the tea.

8. If tea is left standing in the pot for longer than 30 minutes make a fresh pot.

boiling water then becomes merely hot and the full delicious flavour is only partially released; and do take the teapot to the kettle! Use one teaspoonful per person and one for the pot. Leave the tea to infuse. Not less than three minutes and longer with a larger leaf.

"Sugar or other sweeteners can be added to taste. The addition of milk is usual with the full-bodied Indian and Ceylon teas whilst a slice of lemon is often preferred in the more delicate China teas. An excellent brew of tea can also be made using tea bags. These are convenient in that they save the tiresome chore of emptying tea leaves from the pot and are ideal for a single cup."

On that last point, the Tea Board of India recommends that tea-bags, and all other tea for that matter. must always be brewed in a teapot, not a cup, "if you want the true flavour. You must begin with fresh, merrily bubbling, boiling water; just 'very hot' water *will not do*. You must have fiercely boiling water to extract the goodness and flavour from the tea leaves, but do not overboil. If water is kept boiling for some time it becomes de-aerated. Tea made from such water does not have a 'live' taste. You must use 'enough' tea. For *hot* tea, 'enough' is one tea-bag or one teaspoon of tea per cup. For iced tea you will need to use half again as much as for *hot* tea, to allow for the melting of the ice.

"You must pour the boiling water directly over the tea leaves, because water temperature drops so very fast that only by pouring the still bubbling water immediately over the tea can you make the leaves produce their true flavour. The golden rule is to take the tea-pot to the kettle, not the kettle to the tea-pot. Now let your tea brew — never boil — for no less than three minutes, no more than five minutes by the clock. Stir and serve. Some tea drinkers don't like to watch the clock, they prefer to brew tea by guess or by colour. As a result they rarely have good tea, because if you guess three minutes you are almost certain to be one minute out.

If taking the teapot to the boiling water sounds a bit confusing, Samuel Twining himself has often quoted his "five golden rules" for tea-making which simplify the process a bit. 1. Use only good quality tea — one teaspoonful per cup plus an extra one for the pot. 2. Use fresh, cold water from the tap. 3. The water should just be allowed to reach boiling point. 4. Warm up the clean teapot. 5. Let the tea brew for five minutes and then stir before serving.

Jacksons, on the other hand, put it all this way: "Keep your tea in a closed container, because tea absorbs extraneous smells and can also lose its own delicate flavour. Always use freshly drawn boiling water. Just hot or just over-boiled water makes a very 'dead' brew. Warm the pot (a brown earthenware or china pot is best) otherwise your

"If you go by colour you are likely to miss again by a minute or more, because some teas colour up almost immediately. But if your tea has brewed from three to five minutes it is bound to have good colour and be a perfect cup of tea as well. Perhaps you are one of those who prefer weak tea; you must still follow the rules for making hearty tea and then weaken it with hot water after the true flavour has been brought out by proper brewing. You should never make weak tea by using less tea or brewing it for under three minutes, if you are to enjoy the full delicious flavour of tea."

It's all so simple. Isn't it?

It's this passion, this complexity of tastes, techniques and commandments that is perhaps the greatest exotica of the illustrious story of tea. This, and the very characteristics that tea has imbued in the dedicated tea drinker. Katharine Whitehorn condemns tea as a "national blight" on the British character. James Laver, in his enjoyable introduction to *The House of Twining*, views this phenomenon in far more John Bull-ish terms:

"Under its benign influence," he declares, "we have attained in this country to something of the Confucian spirit, a readiness to give and take, an unwillingness to push any argument to its conclusion. We are surely the least quarrelsome of all the nations of the earth, and in this happy consummation the tea-table has undoubtedly played its part. We should, therefore, regard as public benefactors those who, during the last couple of centuries, have made it possible for us to refine our passions, steady our nerves, and promote whatever degree of civilisation we may be supposed to have reached by the aid of a 'nice cup of tea'."

The culinar

In many parts of today's tea-drinking world, tea is not only a good companion to food, it is also a food itself. In Manchuria and most of the northern reaches of China and Inner Mongolia, mutton is the staple diet and, because of a scarcity of vegetables and greenstuffs, tea is taken for its digestive qualities and its vitamins — it's rich in vitamins B1, B2, C and P and is a plentiful source of folic and nicotinic acid.

The Burmese not only drink tea, they eat it too. The tea leaf, which they often call the "Leaf of the Gods," is pickled by mixing fruit with it, then left for a week or two, tightly packed, to ferment. Before it is served, oil, powdered dried shrimps, fried garlic, fried monkey nuts, fried coconut slices and roasted peas are added. The result is not only a common meal but also an essential ingredient of social custom. At one time the Burmese considered an engaged couple to be married once they'd eaten pickled tea from the same dish.

If that seems horrifying to Western tastes, it's worth remembering that the early American pioneers of the tea cult were not sure whether tea was to be drunk or eaten, and there's the story of a Scottish family in the 18th century who, upon receiving their first gift of tea, put it in a pot, poured boiling water on it, steeped it for a while and then proceeded to eat it as if it was a vegetable.

The Tibetans relish a tea-meal called *tjampa* — a mass of ground rice or beans worked into a paste with buttered tea. In India, tea has traditionally been infused with fragrant spices, and is often boiled with rich buffalo milk to make a delicious "masala" tea. In Kashmir, a green fragrant tea is still made in silver samovars, infused with ginger, almonds, cinnamon and cardomoms. Canada's Eskimos are said to like their tea strong and very sweet, and "they don't mind chewing the leaves."[1]

The Japanese also cook with tea, and one of their most popular lunchtime snacks is *Chazuke* (Japanese rice with green tea) in which an aromatic, smoky green tea is poured over a bowl of precooked rice topped with flaked fish and special seasonings.

To most Chinese, tea is more a table companion, especially in the South where the tradition of serving *dim sum* delicacies, or hors d'oeuvres, with tea began as far back as the Sung dynasty when cooks of the imperial households created them to whet the pampered appetites of their emperors. The fashion spread North, where, since those ancient times, *dim sum* styles have focused on buns and dumplings made with wheat flour, staple food of the northerners. In the South, thin rice flour pastries contain finely chopped chicken and barbecued pork, and other *dim sum* treats include small meatballs, a wide range of prawn and shrimp preparations, stewed pork, noodles and sweet dishes. After the Mongolian conquest of China in the Yuan dynasty, tea and its accompanying "vices" were banned from the courts and remained out of favour right through the reign of the Mongol emperors. The Ming rulers restored tea to its supremacy as a beverage, put the *dim sum* back into the mainstream of Chinese cuisine and even enlivened it with more exotic tidbits.

Just as nowadays you can find a Chinese restaurant just about anywhere in any Western country, so can you find *dim sum*. New York and San Francisco have plenty of *dim sum* eating houses, while London's Li Ho Fook Restaurant offers a range of "dot hearts," as the Chinese name for the meal translates, which compare with the best you'll find in Hong Kong. Australian Chinese food fanatics visit Sydney's Tai Ping or Melbourne's Yum Cha restaurants. And for those who prefer to cook at home, modern food technology now makes it possible to turn out tasty *dim sum* in minutes in the average kitchen. Two major food exporters in Hong Kong produce frozen *dim sum* which are marketed in major cities right around the world, and the quality is surprisingly good. Naturally, *dim sum* go best with Chinese teas — the black Po Erh and Keemun, the oolongs like the popular Wu-I Shui Hsien and the Jasmine and Dragon Well greens. If there's not a Chinese food produce store in your district, both Twinings and Jacksons market China blends that lend themselves well to *dim sum*. In Hong Kong, one of the most famous *dim sum* restaurants is Lok Yu in Stanley Street, Central, named after the great grandfather of tea himself, Lu Yu. The Lok Yu has been catering to tea and *dim sum* lovers for nearly 50 years, and though it's been moved from its original location in Wing Kut Lane, it has retained its traditional old Ming dynasty

connection

charm of blackwood furniture, engraved stained-glass partitions and splendid wall hangings with inscriptions from Lu Yu's "Ch'a Ch'ing," *The Tea Classic*.

Tea also provides for some inventive interpretation in Chinese cuisine. Tea leaves are used to produce a fragrant smoke, with camphor wood, to produce smoked duck, a speciality of Szechwan province. A decorative dish of boiled eggs calls for the shells to be "crazed" and the eggs steeped in a strong infusion of tea to produce a fine tracework of lines on the ivory-white hard yolks. A subtly seasoned seafood dish is made with crystal (pale white) prawns fried on green tea leaves in the Shanghai tradition.

Throughout the European and Anglo-Saxon world, much blander tastes generally reign, and tea has traditionally been purely an accompaniment — essential though it is — to full meals or teatime snacks ranging from thinly sliced cucumber, water cress and boiled egg on brown bread to rich cakes and cream-filled sponges and scones. There are a few off-beat exceptions: Says James Laver, "In the north of England they take it with cockles and even with cold tripe," and in Australia, where a particularly strong brew is favoured, medical authorities have been concerned for some years about a particularly dangerous fashion among suburban house-bound women of taking breakfasts consisting entirely of tea and analgesic powders — the constant and increasing abuse of the analgesics being one reason for a growing incidence of kidney disease and malfunction among

Australians.

Iced tea has been a national beverage in America since it was introduced at the World's Fair in St Louis in 1904. In the northern states, hot tea is taken in winter in much the same fashion as it's drunk in Britain. "Americans like their tea to keep pouring during a meal and they prefer to have their croissants, scones and sweet rolls served hot, not cold from the cart as is the British custom. In Ireland, tea comes to the table at breakfast with bacon, sausage, poached eggs, soda bread, butter and marmalade. And at the midnight hour, a tea cart may roll in with homemade fruitcake."[2] The Scots go for shortbreads, gingerbread, hot rolls, currant bread; the Lancashiremen sometimes spike their tea with rum or Scotch whisky on a cold morning. But ever since the days of the 19th century Duchess of Bedford, tea, to the British, has been most associated with the genteel, gossipy yet discreet Afternoon Tea. Its ingredients have long been established as neatly sliced, wafer-thin sandwiches with biscuits and, for the sweet tooth, maybe a deliciously light Victoria Sponge Sandwich Cake, light as a feather and sweetened with a filling of raspberry jam, a Battenburg Cake encased with sweet marzipan icing, or a Dundee Cake, a rich fruit and nut filled affair adopted from the Scottish kitchen and excellent as a christening, wedding or Christmas cake. A later tradition, very popular today, has been Cream Teas combining milky hot tea with freshly baked scones filled with whipped cream and strawberry or raspberry jam. In certain areas very slightly sour clotted cream is used.

The Duchess's original rules of etiquette have long presided over the drawing rooms of Britain, and though battling with changing tastes today they are surviving in some households. The perfect Afternoon Tea should be served in the drawing room, by a fire in winter and with the blinds drawn in summer. A small round table should be set with a delicate afternoon tea tablecloth, either plain white or embroidered but certainly only of the best linen. Each place should be set with a small plate and knife, a cup and saucer and sugar spoon. The tea equipage itself should be in silver with matching pot, hot water jug, sugar bowl, milk jug and tongs. The most acceptable tea service — cups and saucers — would be fine bone china. Sugar would be in small white lumps. Each guest would have a small linen napkin. Sandwiches would be served on sandwich plates lined with lace doilies, cakes and biscuits from a three-tiered cake-stand. Conversation should be light, and table manners exquisite.

Of course, refined afternoon teas are fighting a losing battle against the steadily increasing pace and pressures of 20th century life. According to an American newspaper report, even afternoon tea at London's Dorchester Hotel — named by *The Times* several years ago as representing "the pinnacle of tea-making" — has lost a few points on the Duchess of Bedford's strict list of do's and don'ts. To judge what it called "the current standards of afternoon tea" in London, the newspaper sent a reporter off to the Dorchester "at the appropriate hour" with two English matrons. This is what the newspaper concluded:

"All Englishwomen seem to know everything about tea. The first thing they say is that the very last place in England to find a good afternoon tea — that is, the tea itself and everything that goes with it — is London. In the north, the tradition is stronger and the food better. In the southwest, thick 'clotted' cream and homemade strawberry jam are featured, and the whole spread is called cream tea. The thick cream goes on the biscuits, not in the tea.

"Nevertheless, the Dorchester looks the part this particular afternoon. In its colonnaded foyer, low tables are covered with linen and set with china. The waiters, attired in black tie and tails, are suitably deferential. The tea arrives in a silver service accompanied by the traditional bite-sized sandwiches and miniature French pastries.

"But standards do seem to be slipping. The women point out that paper napkins have replaced proper linen ones. What's more, the sandwiches contain salmon paste instead of smoked salmon and — horror of horrors — *there is a tea bag in the silver pot.*"

Aside from afternoon teas, the Anglo-Saxon blend of tea and food is a pretty indiscriminate affair, though the major speciality tea producers are trying to educate the average Briton, Australian and American in at least what types of tea should go with different dishes. Earl Grey goes well with fish dishes, for example; Darjeeling is a good accompaniment for curry and Orange Pekoe should be drunk with kebabs and pilaffs. Earl Grey and Jasmine are best for sweetmeats, and with Chinese and Japanese food it would be beyond the bounds of good taste to drink anything but Chinese and Japanese teas — the lapsang souchongs, jasmines and green gunpowders.

CUCUMBER SANDWICHES

Butter very thinly sliced white bread and remove crusts. Arrange on it thinly sliced peeled cucumber and sprinkle with salt. Cover with another slice of buttered bread, and cut diagonally into quarters.

MUSTARD AND CRESS AND EGG SANDWICHES

Butter very thinly sliced brown bread and arrange on it chopped hard-boiled egg. Cover with a layer of fresh mustard and cress. Cover with another slices of buttered brown bread and cut diagonally into quarters.

SCONES

500 g/1 lb	self-raising flour
1 tsp	salt
60 g/2 oz	butter
315 ml/1¼ cups	buttermilk

Sieve the flour and salt into a mixing bowl and rub in the butter until the mixture is finely crumbed. Add buttermilk, work in well, then knead to a soft dough.

Flour a pastry board and roll out or press the dough out to 1.25-2cm (½-¾″) thick. Cut out rounds with a 5-6.25cm (2-2½″) pastry cutter. Brush tops with milk and bake on a lightly greased and floured baking sheet in a moderately hot over, at 200°C/400°F, until well risen and golden brown, about 12 minutes.

Slice in half and serve with butter and strawberry or raspberry jam. Replace butter with whipped or clotted cream to serve as part of the 'Cream Tea'.

VICTORIA SPONGE SANDWICH

The classic recipe for this light and airy sponge cake calls for the weight of the separate ingredients — flour, sugar and butter — to each amount to the weight of the eggs.

3	eggs (about 185 g/6 oz)
185 g/6 oz	butter
185 g/6 oz	sugar
185 g/6 oz	self-raising flour
½ tsp	salt
	milk

Cream the butter and sugar together, then add the beaten eggs by degrees until the mixture is light and creamy. Sieve flour with salt onto the batter and stir in.

Add just enough milk to make a soft batter of dropping consistency. Pour into two lightly greased and floured 18 cm/7″ sandwich tins, lined with greased and floured greaseproof paper.

Bake in a moderate oven, 180°C/350°F, for 30 minutes, or until a skewer comes out clean when inserted in the centre of the cakes. Turn out onto a cake rack.

When cold, sandwich with raspberry jam or sweetened whipped cream. Dust the top with sifted icing sugar.

BATTENBURG CAKE

Prepare the Victoria Sponge Sandwich batter. Line a rectangular 23cm x 12.5cm/9″ x 5″ baking tin with a sheet of aluminium foil, making a firm division down the centre, lengthways.

Colour one half of the batter yellow, the remaining half pink and pour the separate batters into the two sections of the tin.

Bake in the same way as Victoria Sponge Sandwich.

Remove to a cake rack to cool, then cut each piece along its length, into two. Join the four cakes together with apricot jam into a chequer-patterned block and cover the entire cake with a thick marzipan, after brushing generously with apricot jam.

Crimp the edges of the marzipan and score the top with a lattice pattern.

To make marzipan use:

375 g/¾ lb	finely ground almonds
185 g/6 oz	caster sugar
1	egg
1 tsp	orange flower water
	juice of 1 small lemon
	almond essence

Mix the dry ingredients together, then add the beaten egg, flower water, lemon juice and almond essence. Work to a smooth paste. Roll out to a large enough rectangular shape to completely encase the cake.

DUNDEE CAKE

250 g/½ lb	butter
220 g/7 oz	sugar
5	eggs
315 g/10 oz	all-purpose flour
125 g/¼ lb	currants
125 g/¼ lb	raisins
125 g/¼ lb	candied peel
10	glace cherries
	grated rind of 1 orange
125 g/¼ lb	finely ground almonds
½ tsp	salt
½ tsp	baking powder
1 tbsp	milk
60 g/2 oz	blanched slivered almonds

Cream the butter and sugar, then beat eggs and add slowly to the butter cream, alternating with the sieved flour. Beat thoroughly. Stir in washed, dried and lightly floured currants, raisins and chopped peel. Add halved glace cherries and orange rind, ground almonds and salt. Mix baking powder with milk and stir into the batter, mixing thoroughly.

Pour into a prepared 20 cm/8″ deep-sided cake tin lined with greaseproof paper. Arrange the almonds on top and bake in a preheated slow oven, 150°C/300°F, for 1½ hours. Test with a thin skewer.

Leave the cake to cool in the tin, then turn out onto a cake rack.

DROP SCONES

(Makes 24)

500 g/1 lb	self-raising flour
4 tbsp	sugar
½ tsp	salt
2 tbsp	warmed golden or corn syrup
315 ml/1¼ cups	buttermilk
2	eggs, beaten

Sieve the flour into a mixing bowl, add sugar, salt and syrup and mix lightly. Add the buttermilk and beaten eggs and beat to a smooth batter of dropping consistency.

Wipe a well-heated iron griddle or frying pan with a greased cloth and pour on tablespoonfuls of the mixture, keeping well separated. Cook until the surface bubbles and the undersides are lightly browned. Flip over and cook the other sides. Lift out and keep warm by wrapping in a clean kitchen towel.

When all are cooked, serve warm (or serve cold) with butter and jam or honey.

SCOTS CRUMPETS (TEA PANCAKES)

250 g/½ lb	all-purpose flour
1 tsp	salt
3 tbsp	caster sugar
2	eggs
3 tbsp	melted butter
375 ml/1½ cups	buttermilk

Sieve the flour and salt into a mixing bowl and add sugar. Stir lightly. Beat eggs well and add to the mixture with the melted butter. Pour in buttermilk slowly, beating until the batter is of a thin pouring consistency, similar to thin cream.

Wipe out a well-warmed griddle or iron frying pan with a greased cloth and pour in enough batter to cover the pan in a thin layer. Turn the pan so the batter spreads evenly. Set over moderate heat and cook until the underside is golden and the surface bubbling. Flip over and cook the other side. Lift out and keep warm by wrapping in a clean kitchen cloth.

Serve warm, spread with butter and jam or honey and rolled up.

SHORTBREAD

500 g/1 lb	all-purpose flour
500 g/1 lb	self-raising flour
500 g/1 lb	butter
250 g/½ lb	caster sugar
½ tsp	salt

Cream the butter and sugar together, then add the sieved flours and work in very lightly with the salt, until the mixture is of a soft, crumbly texture. Do not overwork or the biscuit will become tough.

Place on an ungreased baking sheet and shape into a smooth, round cake. Pinch the edges with finger and thumb and prick all over with a fork.

Bake in a slow oven at 150°C/300°F, for about 1 hour.

Leave to cool, then turn out onto a rack. It may be dusted with icing sugar before serving.

This Scottish speciality is a favourite festive cake which was originally made with very fine oatmeal.

DANISH TEA CAKE (THEKAGE)

250 g/½ lb	sugar
250 g/½ lb	butter
2	eggs
185 g/6 oz	all-purpose flour
1 tsp	baking powder
	grated rind of 1 lemon
6 tbsp	boiling water
	lemon icing
	chocolate granules

Beat the sugar and butter until creamy. Add eggs separately, beating well, then add the sieved flour, baking powder and lemon rind. Mix well. Stir in the boiling water and quickly mix, then immediately pour into a prepared baking tin with a detachable bottom lined with well-greased greaseproof paper.

Bake in a preheated moderately hot oven at 200°C/400°F, for 1 hour. Turn out and leave to cool, then decorate with lemon icing and sprinkle on chocolate granules.

SHAO MAI (STEAMED MEAT DUMPLINGS)

(Makes 24)

24 pieces	frozen or fresh wonton wrappers*
185 g/6 oz	semi-fat pork
90 g/3 oz	raw prawns or shrimp, shelled
60 g/2 oz	canned water chestnuts, drained
1 tbsp	light soy sauce
2 tsp	sugar
½ tsp	salt
2 tsp	cornflour
2 tsp	vegetable oil

Thaw frozen wonton wrappers and cover with a damp cloth until needed. Coarsely mince pork, prawns or shrimp and water chestnuts and mix with the seasonings.

Place a spoonful in the centre of each wrapper and fold the wrapper up around the filling. Press into a squared shape, flattening the base. Leave the top open.

Arrange the dumplings in a lightly greased steaming basket, or on an oiled plate. Set in a steamer over boiling water, cover and steam for 10 minutes.

Serve with dipping sauces of soy and hot mustard or chilli sauce.

*Note: Wonton wrappers are available at Oriental provisions stores.

SPRING ROLLS
(Makes 12)

12 sheets	Chinese frozen spring roll wrappers*
185 g/6 oz	lean pork tenderloin, or chicken
4	Chinese black mushrooms, soaked
90 g/3 oz	canned bamboo shoot, drained
½ medium	onion
1 tbsp	light soy sauce
1 tsp	sugar
½ tsp	salt
2 tsp	cornflour
2 tbsp	vegetable oil
	deep-frying oil

Thaw the spring roll wrappers, then cover with a damp cloth and set aside until needed.

Cut the meat into thin shreds. Drain mushroom, remove stem and shred.

Cut the bamboo shoot into juliennes. Thinly slice the onion.

Mix meat with soy sauce, sugar, salt and cornflour.

Heat the vegetable oil in a frying pan and when very hot fry the meat, stirring continuously, over high heat for 2 minutes. Add the onion, mushroom and bamboo shoot and continue to cook, stirring, until the onion is cooked through. Remove from the heat and leave to cool.

Place a large spoonful of the mixture in the centre of a spring roll wrapper. Fold in one corner, diagonally, then two sides. Fold the final flap around the roll and stick down with water.

Prepare all the spring rolls in this way.

Heat deep-frying oil to very hot, then reduce temperature slightly.

Fry the rolls, several at a time, to a golden-brown. Remove and drain well.

Serve hot with Worcestershire sauce.

*Note: Spring Roll wrappers are available at Oriental provisions stores and some supermarkets.

CHIAO TZE
(STEAMED MEAT DUMPLINGS)
(Makes 48)

Pastry:	
250 g/½ lb	all-purpose flour
200 ml/¾ cup	cold water
½ tsp	salt
Filling:	
375 g/¾ lb	semi-fat pork
250 g/½ lb	white cabbage
1 tbsp	light soy sauce
2 tsp	sugar
½ tsp	salt
2 tsp	vegetable oil

Sieve the flour into a mixing bowl, add cold water and salt and mix together. Knead to make a smooth, fairly stiff dough.

Finely mince the pork and finely chop cabbage. Mix together, adding the seasonings and vegetable oil.

Divide the dough into four and cover three parts with a damp cloth.

Roll out the other part into a paper thin sheet, on a lightly floured board. Using a 6cm/2½″ pastry cutter, divide the pastry into 12 circular pieces.

Place a spoonful of the filling in the centre of each wrapper and fold over. Pinch the edges together, using a little milk or water to seal.

Prepare the remaining dough and fillings and when all are done, arrange on a cabbage leaf in a bamboo steaming basket or on an oiled plate.

Set in a steamer over boiling water. Cover and steam for 10 minutes.

Serve with a dip of light soy sauce.

PAKORAS
(FRIED VEGETABLE DUMPLINGS)
(Makes 36)

185 g/6 oz	cauliflower
1	green capsicum
1	fresh red chilli
1 large	onion
185 g/6 oz	all-purpose flour
185 g/6 oz	ground rice or rice powder
30 g/1 oz	fine semolina (optional)
2 tsp	salt
1-2 tsp	chilli powder
1 tsp	mixed spice
¾ tsp	turmeric powder
1 tbsp	chopped parsley
	deep-frying oil

Grate the cauliflower, then squeeze it hard to remove as much water as possible. Set aside. Finely chop capsicum, chilli and onion and mix with cauliflower the flour, rice powder, semolina and seasonings.

Add cold water gradually, beating well, until a thick batter is formed.

Heat the deep-frying oil in a large pan and drop in spoonfuls of the batter. Fry until they are golden-brown and crisp on the surface.

Remove and drain well.

Serve with mango or mint chutney.

SAMOOSAS (POTATO TURNOVERS)
(Makes 24)

Pastry:	
185 g/6oz	all-purpose flour
½ tsp	salt
15 g/½ oz	butter
155 ml/⅝ cup	milk
	deep-frying oil
Stuffing:	
500 g/1 lb	potatoes
1	small onion
1½ tsp	salt
½-1 tsp	chilli powder

½ tsp	mixed spice
1 tbsp	chopped parsley
2 tsp	lemon juice
30 g/1 oz	butter

Sieve the flour and salt into a mixing bowl. Make a well in the centre and add the melted butter, then milk which has been heated to lukewarm. Mix well, then knead into a stiff pastry. Cover with a damp cloth and set aside.

Boil potatoes in their jackets. Cool and peel. Mash, working until they are quite smooth. Chop onion finely.

Melt the butter in a frying pan and fry onion very gently for about 5 minutes, until cooked but not coloured. Add potatoes and remaining filling ingredients and mix well. Cook, stirring, until the mixture is dry, then remove from the heat. Leave to cool.

Divide the pastry into 24 equal parts and roll each out into a round as thin as possible.

Place a spoonful of the filling in the centre of each. Damp the edges with milk and fold into a half-circle. Press the edges together and crimp with the fingers.

Deep-fry slowly in moderately hot oil, turning several times. When golden brown, remove and drain well.

Serve very hot with mint chutney or a spicy tomato sauce.

SHAKAR PARAS

185 g/6 oz	all-purpose flour
30 g/1 oz	butter
30 g/1 oz	ground almonds
4 tbsp	milk
125 g/¼ lb	white sugar
2 tbsp	water
	shallow-frying oil

Sieve the flour into a mixing bowl and make a well in the centre.

Pour in melted butter and add the ground almonds.

Warm the milk and pour in, working into the flour until the dough is smooth and stiff. Knead well, then roll out to a thickness of about 1cm, just over ¼″. Cut into bite-size squares.

Boil the sugar and water together until it begins to thicken and change colour. Remove from the heat, but keep warm.

Heat shallow oil to moderately hot and fry the squares until lightly coloured. Lift out and drain well. Dip into the syrup and arrange on a lightly greased plate.

Pour on the remaining syrup which will set into a toffee coating.

Break apart when cool.

GLACE CREME AU THE
(Serves 8-10)

250 g/½ lb	fine sugar
8	egg yolks
700 ml/2¾ cups	boiling milk
2 tbsp	good black or scented tea leaves

Beat sugar with egg yolks until very smooth and thick. Infuse tea leaves in the boiling milk for 5 minutes, then strain into the batter and stir in a double saucepan until the mixture is of coating consistency. Do not allow it to boil.

Remove from the heat and pour into dessert cups and stir from time to time until firm, then chill.

Decorate with glazed cherries and powdered sugar.

TEA CREAM
(Serves 4)

1 tbsp	good black or scented tea leaves
315 ml/1¼ cups	boiling water
3	egg yolks
90 g/3 oz	fine sugar
	zest of ½ lemon
	zest of 1 orange
2 small glasses	dark rum
	dark rum
5 leaves	gelatine
500 ml/2 cups	whipped cream

Pour the boiling water onto tea leaves and leave to infuse for 4 minutes.

Beat egg yolks with sugar until light and creamy, add the lemon and orange zest with the rum and beat until smooth.

Soak gelatine in a little boiling water and strain into the creamy mixture.

Stir lightly, then add the strained tea liquor and whipped cream.

Fold together lightly.

Fill tall glasses with the cream and leave to set in the refrigerator.

Decorate with crystallised fruit and whipped cream.

TEA ICECREAM
(Serves 6)

6	egg yolks
185 g/6 oz	fine sugar
500 ml/2 cups	single cream
2 tbsp	Earl Grey, Jasmine or other scented tea leaves

Beat egg yolks with sugar until thick and creamy. Rinse a saucepan with cold water and pour in the cream. Heat until nearly boiling, then remove from heat, add tea and infuse, cover for 1 minute.

Pour through a nylon strainer onto the egg mixture, pressing on the leaves to extract as much of the essence as possible.

Beat well, then set pot over simmering water or in a double saucepan and gently beat until beginning to thicken.

Cool, then pour into trays and freeze until set.

When firm, break up and beat again until smooth and fluffy, then return the trays to the freezer.

Remove from the freezer half an hour before serving, but keep refrigerated.

The icecream may be tinted a light pink, green or yellow using food colouring.

LEMON TEA ICECREAM

2 tbsp	lemon flavoured tea leaves
500 ml/2 cups	boiling water
3	egg yolks
125 g/¼ lb	fine sugar
	juice of 1 lemon
	zest of ½ orange
500 ml/2 cups	whipped cream

Infuse the tea leaves in boiling water for 4 minutes.

Beat the egg yolks and sugar together until thick and creamy. Add the lemon juice and orange zest and strain in the lemon tea. Beat well, then fold in the whipped cream. Colour a light yellow with food colouring.

Pour into icecream trays and leave to set in the freezer. Remove, break up and beat again, then refreeze in small dessert cups.

Remove from the freezer half an hour before serving and decorate with whipped cream and pieces of crystallised lemon and orange.

Return to the refrigerator until ready to serve.

TEA SOUFFLE

(Serves 4)

30 g/1 oz	butter
30 g/1 oz	all-purpose flour
3 tbsp	milk
250 ml/1 cup	strong black or scented tea
60 g/2 oz	fine sugar
4	egg yolks
5	egg whites
	pinch salt

Make a roux of butter and flour, stirring on moderate heat. Add the milk to make a stiff paste, then beat in the tea by degrees, stirring until the sauce thickens. Add sugar, stir in well and cook on moderate to low heat, stirring constantly, for 5 minutes. Leave to cool slightly, then add beaten egg yolks.

Whip the whites with salt until firm, but not too stiff.

Prepare a souffle dish, greasing it lightly, then dusting with flour or sugar. Fold egg whites into the sauce. Do not beat or over-stir even if the batter is slightly marbled.

Pour into the prepared dish and bake in a moderately hot oven at 200°C/400°F until well risen, about 20 minutes for individual souffles, longer for a single larger one.

It should be golden on top, well risen, but soft and even liquid in the middle.

Dust with sifted icing sugar and glaze under a very hot grill immediately before serving.

TEA JELLY

1 package	lemon flavoured jelly
425 ml/1¾ cups	fresh black tea
	grated rind of 2 lemons
	lemon slices
	whipped cream

Dissolve the jelly in half the boiling hot tea, then cool.

When it begins to thicken add remaining tea and the lemon rind.

Pour into wetted individual moulds and leave to set, then chill.

Decorate with thinly slices lemon and whipped cream.

TEA TRUFFLES

60 g/2 oz	butter
2	egg yolks
125 g/¼ lb	icing sugar
3 heaped tbsp	scented tea leaves
125 ml/½ cup	boiling water
	zest of ½ orange
375 g/¾ lb	piping chocolate
	sweetened cocoa powder

Beat eggs with butter until smooth and creamy, then work in the icing sugar and beat until smooth. Infuse the tea in boiling water and leave for 4 minutes, then strain into the butter cream. Add orange zest and melted chocolate and mix well.

Spread onto a greased tray to a thickness of 1.25cm/½″ and leave to set. Cut into small squares and coat thickly with the cocoa powder.

TEA BRACK

This is a traditional Irish loaf cake which combines dried fruits marinated in tea and whisky with a cake batter laced with spices. The original version of this cake was made with yeast.

185 g/6 oz	sultanas
185 g/6 oz	raisins
185 g/6 oz	brown sugar
225 ml/³⁄₄ cup	strong black tea
75 ml/¼ cup	Irish Whisky
185 g/6 oz	all-purpose flour
2	eggs, beaten
1 tsp	baking powder
1 tsp	mixed spice
1 tbsp	slivered almonds

Wash sultanas and raisins and dry well. Place in a bowl, cover with sugar and pour on the tea and Whisky. Cover and leave for 24 hours.

Stir in sieved flour, eggs, baking powder, spices and the almonds and mix well.

Pour into a greased and lightly floured 20 x 10cm/8 x 4″ loaf tin.

Bake in a preheated moderate oven at 150°C, 300°F for 1¼-1½ hours.

When cooked, remove from the oven and leave to cool in the tin, then remove and brush with honey to glaze.

NEW ZEALAND LAMB CHOPS BRAISED IN TEA

4 large	shoulder lamb chops
1 medium	onion, sliced
1 clove	garlic, sliced
250 ml/1 cup	cold black tea
Sauce:	
125 ml/½ cup	mayonnaise
½ tsp	white vinegar
½ tsp	salt
1 tsp	horseradish sauce
2 tsp	chopped mint or mint sauce

Trim the chops and place in a casserole with onion and garlic. Pour on the tea. Cover and braise over moderate heat, turning once, until chops are tender and tea evaporated, about 40 minutes.

Uncover the pan in last stages of cooking to brown the chops.

Mix the sauce ingredients together, beating well.

Place the chops on a serving plate and pour a serving of sauce onto each one. Serve at once.

SALMON ON RICE WITH JAPANESE GREEN TEA

125 g/¼ lb	poached or canned salmon
2 tbsp	light soy sauce
2 tbsp	sake or semi-sweet sherry
750 g/1½ lb	cooked white rice (hot)
740 ml/3 cups	fresh Japanese green tea
3 tbsp	white sesame seeds

Flake the salmon and marinate in a frying pan with the soy sauce and sherry for 10 minutes. Place on moderate heat and simmer until the sauces have been absorbed.

Roast the sesame seeds in a dry frying pan over moderately low heat until they begin to jump. Remove from the heat.

Divide rice between six bowls and top with a serving of the salmon.

Sprinkle on sesame seeds.

Two minutes before serving pour in the boiling hot tea. Cover the bowls.

CAMPHOR WOOD AND TEA SMOKED DUCK

(Chinese)

1	duck (about 2 kg/4 lb)
3 tbsp	salt
2 tsp	black peppercorns, ground
2 tsp	Chinese five spices powder
1 tbsp	light soy sauce
2 cups	camphor wood chips
½ cup	black tea leaves
1 piece	dried tangerine peel (or orange peel)
	deep-frying oil

Roast the salt and pepper in a dry frying pan over moderately low heat for about 2 minutes. Remove from the heat and mix in the five spices powder and leave to cool.

Clean and wash the duck and dry carefully. Drain any liquid from the cavity. Rub the salt mixture well into the skin and inside the duck and leave for about 8 hours to absorb the seasonings.

Hang the duck, by tying a string around the neck, in an airy place for a further 6-8 hours until the skin is fairly dry.

Place the camphor wood chips, black tea leaves and tangerine peel in the bottom of a large saucepan and set on a fairly high fire. Place a wire rack in the pan and put the duck on this. Cover and smoke over low heat for about 10 minutes. Turn the duck and smoke for 7 minutes longer. It should be quite brown.

Place on a lightly oiled plate and steam for 2 hours, until very tender.

Heat deep-frying oil to very hot. Make sure there is no liquid in the cavity of the duck. Lower the duck into the oil and deep-fry, basting constantly with the hot oil, until it is deep-brown and crispy.

Remove and drain well.

Cut into bite-size pieces.

To serve, wrap several slices of duck, a piece of spring onion and a teaspoonful of sweet barbecue sauce in a lettuce leaf or savoury pancake.

STIR-FRIED SHRIMPS WITH JASMINE TEA LEAVES

375 g/¾ lb	medium sized shrimps, shelled
3 tbsp	jasmine tea leaves
2 tsp	light soy sauce
2 tsp	dry sherry
1 tsp	sugar
3 tbsp	vegetable oil

Remove the dark veins from shrimps and wash very well. Wipe dry with a kitchen towel.

Soak jasmine leaves in boiling water until softened, then drain.

Reserve about 4 tablespoons of the liquor.

Heat the vegetable oil in a wok or frying pan and fry the shrimps, stirring continually, for 1 minute. Add the soy sauce, sherry and sugar and mix well, then put in the tea leaves.

Stir all together for about ½ minute on the high heat, then pour in the reserved tea liquor and cook until most of the liquid has evaporated.

Serve immediately with white rice.

TEA SMOKED PEKING CHICKEN

1	spring chicken (about 1¼ kg/2½ lb)
1 tsp	black peppercorns, ground
2 tsp	Chinese five spices powder
2 tbsp	coarse salt
2	spring onions
4 slices	fresh root ginger
2	star anise
1 pc	cinnamon bark
250 ml/1 cup	dark soy sauce
90 g/3 oz	sugar
60 g/2 oz	all-purpose flour or ground rice
4 tbsp	black tea leaves
1 tbsp	sesame oil or vegetable oil

Clean the chicken and wipe dry. Roast the peppercorns with coarse salt in a dry frying pan for 2 minutes on moderately low heat. Remove and grind finer, then add the five spices powder. When cool rub into the chicken.

Place the chicken in a saucepan and cover with boiling water. Add the spring onions, ginger, star anise and cinnamon bark. Bring to the boil and simmer for 20 minutes, turning once.

Lift out and drain very well.

Place sugar, flour or rice and black tea leaves in the bottom of a large saucepan and set a wire rack over them. Place over high heat until they begin to smoke, then put in the chicken and reduce the heat. Cover and smoke on each side for 7 minutes.

Remove and rub with the sesame or vegetable oil.

Cut into bite-size pieces and serve hot or cold.

CHINESE MARBLED TEA EGGS

12	eggs
1½ tbsp	salt
4 tbsp	black Chinese tea leaves
3	star anise
1 piece	cinnamon stick

Hard-boil the eggs for 8 minutes, then drain and cover with cold water for 3 minutes. Drain again.

Gently tap the shells all around, until the eggshells are marbled with small cracks.

Put salt, tea leaves and spices into a saucepan with about 1½ lit/6 cups water. Bring to the boil.

Add eggs, reduce heat and simmer for at least 1 hour.

Drain well, then peel and serve cold with a dish of salt.

ORANGE TEA DESSERT

6-8 dried	Chinese red dates
125 g/4 oz	canned Mandarin oranges
625 ml/2½ cups	liquor from canned Mandarin oranges
	white sugar

Soak dates in boiling water until soft. Drain. Bring the canned liquor to the boil and add sugar. Stir until dissolved. Add dates and Mandarin orange segments. Heat through.

Serve hot or cold.

Use fresh oranges, pineapple, canned pears or apricots in place of the Mandarin oranges for variety.

ALMOND TEA

185 g/6 oz	almonds
220 g/7 oz	white sugar
1¾ litres/7 cups	boiling water
2 tbsp	cornflour
3 tbsp	cold water

Boil the almonds until the skins loosen, then drain. Rub off skins and place the almonds in a blender with 2 cups boiling water. Blend at high speed until the mixture is smooth and creamy. Pour into a saucepan, add sugar and remaining boiling water. Bring to the boil then reduce heat and simmer for 20 minutes. Strain into another saucepan through a fine nylon strainer or a piece of muslin.

Mix cornflour and cold water and pour into the almond mixture.

Bring to the boil and simmer until slightly thickened.

Serve the almond tea hot or cool, in small porcelain bowls.

SWEET TEA EGGS

6	chicken eggs
250 g/½ lb	white sugar
1 litre/4 cups	boiling water

Hard-boil the eggs for 8 minutes, then drain and cover with cold water for 3 minutes. Drain again and remove shells.

Mix sugar with boiling water and stir until dissolved.

Place one egg into each of six dessert bowls and pour in the syrup.

Serve hot or warm.

Dried or candied lotus seeds, white fungus or dried fruit may be boiled in the syrup for extra flavour.

GINGER TEA

10cm/4″ piece	fresh root ginger
	boiling water

Peel and thinly slice the root ginger and rinse.

Place in a teapot and pour on boiling water. Leave to infuse for 5 minutes.

Sweetened, if preferred, with a little white sugar.

Serve as a pick-me-up or after seafood.

BLACKCURRANT TEA

1 heaped tbsp	blackcurrant jam
250 ml/½ cup	boiling water

Simmer together for 5 minutes, then strain.

Add a squeeze of lemon and sugar to taste.

Serve very hot for a cold or sore throat.

LEMON, LIME OR ORANGE TEA

Cut fairly thick slices of the fruit, two for each tall glass.

Place in the glasses and pour on a splash of boiling water to release the full flavour and the oils from the fruit.

Top up with normal strength black tea and add liquid sugar to taste.

MINT TEA, MOROCCAN STYLE

Prepare green tea using Chinese "Gunpowder" of normal strength.

Pour into tall glasses over sprigs of washed fresh mint, and add sugar to taste.

MINT TEA, CEYLON STYLE

Add washed sprigs of fresh mint to tall glasses, splash in a little boiling water and top up with normal strength Ceylon black tea.

Add liquid sugar to taste.

To make iced tea, chill the tea first. Add mint and ice cubes to tall glasses and pour in the tea.

ICED MINT AND LEMON TEA

Squeeze the juice of ½ a lemon into a tall glass. Add sugar to taste and stir to dissolve. Fill the glass with cracked ice and chilled black tea. Stir well and garnish with a sprig of fresh mint.

ICED LEMON TEA

Squeeze the juice of ½ a lemon into a tall glass. Add sugar to taste and stir to dissolve. Fill the glass with cracked ice and chilled black tea. Stir well and garnish with thin slices of lemon.

TEA EVEREST

Fill a glass with ice cubes, add liquid sugar and slivers of fresh fruit, a sprig of basil and strain in cooled black tea.

KASHMIRI SAMOVAR TEA

1½ litres/6 cups	water
750 ml/3 cups	milk
10 tsp	sugar
1.25cm/½″ piece	cinnamon stick
4 pieces	green cardamoms
1 tbsp	green tea leaves
	pinch bicarbonate of soda

Pour water and milk into the outer chamber of the samovar (a jug-like metal vessel with a central chimney set over a container of burning charcoal). Add sugar, spices and green tea and bring to the boil.

Leave to simmer for at least half an hour.

Add bicarbonate of soda to give the tea a pinkish tint and enhance the flavour.

Serve hot.

KAHWA (KASHMIRI TEA)

1 litre/4 cups	water
1½ tsp	green tea leaves
2	green cardamoms, powdered
¼ tsp	powdered cinnamon
3-4	almonds, shredded
	sugar

Bring water to the boil and add tea leaves. Boil for a few minutes and add sugar to taste. Add the spices and almonds and remove from the heat. Cover and serve hot.

SHEER CHA (NORTH INDIAN CREAMY TEA)

1½ litres/6 cups	water
1½ tsp	green tea leaves
375 ml/1½ cups	milk
1 tbsp	cream
	pinch bicarbonate of soda
	salt

Bring water to the boil and add tea leaves with bicarbonate of soda.

Boil for several minutes. Add salt to taste, then add the milk. Boil briefly.

When serving, add the cream.

CARDAMOM TEA

1½ litres/6 cups	water
3 tsp	black tea leaves
3	black cardamoms, peeled
250 ml/1 cup	milk
	sugar

Bring water to the boil and add tea leaves, cardamoms, milk and sugar to taste. Bring back to the boil, then remove from the heat and leave to infuse for 5 minutes before serving.

SPICED TEA (ELAICHA)

1 litre/4 cups	water
1 litre/4 cups	milk
2	cloves
6	green cardamoms
1 small stick	cinnamon
1 round tbsp	black tea leaves
	sugar

Bring water and milk to the boil, together. Add spices and tea leaves and simmer for 1 minute. Remove from the heat, cover and leave for at least 5 minutes. Add sugar to taste and serve hot.

TEA AND FRUIT DRINKS

Mix canned fruit juice, or the liquor from canned fruits, with black tea. Add liquid sugar to taste. Pour into tall glasses over ice cubes and decorate with fresh fruit.

ICED TEA PUNCH

(For 12)

315 ml/1¼ cups	strong black tea
185 g/6 oz	white sugar
315 ml/1¼ cups	orange squash
4 tbsp	lemon juice
2 small bottles	ginger ale
1 large bottle	lemonade
1	orange, sliced

Pour tea into a bowl and add the sugar. Stir until dissolved, then chill. Add orange squash and lemon juice and just before serving pour in the ginger ale and lemonade. Decorate the glasses with orange slices and pour the punch over plenty of cracked ice.

ICED TEA FRUIT CUP

(For 12)

125 g/¼ lb	sugar
1¼ litres/5 cups	water
250 ml/1 cup	strong fresh black tea
250 ml/1 cup	orange squash
250 ml/1 cup	lemon squash
250 ml/1 cup	pineapple juice
1 small bottle	lemonade
12 fresh or canned	cherries
2 bananas	bananas, sliced

Boil the sugar with half the water for 5 minutes. Add tea and remaining water and chill, then add the squash and pineapple juice and chill very well. Just before serving add the lemonade and fruit.

Serve in tall glasses over ice.

FRESH FRUIT AND MINT TEA PUNCH

(For 12)

1¼ litres/5 cups	boiling water
1½ tbsp	black tea leaves
185 g/6 oz	white sugar
500 ml/2 cups	lemon squash
750 ml/3 cups	orange squash
60 g/2 oz	strawberries
½	lemon, sliced
½	orange, sliced
	mint leaves

Boil water and pour over the tea. Leave to infuse for 4 minutes.

Stir, strain into a bowl with the sugar and stir until dissolved.

Add lemon and orange squash. When ready to serve, pour over ice cubes in a punch bowl and add sliced fruit and mint.

HOT SPICED LEMONADE TEA PUNCH

(For 12)

2½ litres/10 cups	boiling water
8	cloves
2 sticks	cinnamon
30 g/1 oz	black tea leaves (or jasmine tea leaves)
125 g/¼ lb	white sugar
250 ml/1 cup	orange squash
250 ml/1 cup	pineapple juice
	juice of 2 lemons
	lemon slices
	cloves

Add the cloves and cinnamon to boiling water and bring back to the boil.

Pour in the tea, remove from the heat and infuse for 5 minutes.

Stir and strain into a bowl containing the sugar. Stir until dissolved.

Add the fruit squash and juices.

To reheat before serving, place over low heat, but do not allow to boil.

Decorate with clove-studded lemon slices.

TEA FLIP

(For 2)

315 ml/1¼ cups	boiling milk
2 tsp	black tea leaves
2 tsp	honey
1	egg yolk
2 small glasses	dark rum
	whipped cream
	chocolate shavings

Infuse the tea leaves in the milk. Sweeten with honey and leave for 5 minutes. Strain and stir in lightly beaten egg yolk and the rum.

Pour into glasses and decorate with whipped cream and chocolate shavings.

SPICED HOT TEA PUNCH

(For 12)

1 bottle	good red wine
250 ml/1 cup	dark rum
1	lemon
2	cinnamon sticks
8	cloves
8	sugar cubes
625 ml/2½ cups	boiling water
2½ tbsp	black tea leaves

Heat the wine until just below boiling, then reduce heat slightly.

Add the cinnamon sticks and cloves.

Infuse the tea in boiling water and leave for 5 minutes. Strain over the wine. Pour the rum into a ladle and add the sugar cubes.

Flame, and lower into the punch. Serve while warm.

TEA BORDEAUX

1 bottle	good red Bordeaux wine
equal volume	strong black tea
	sugar syrup
	lemon slices

Prepare fresh tea and pour into the wine. Add sugar and lemon slices and serve at once.

TEA TABLA

(For 1)

250 ml/1 cup	strong black tea
1 measure	dark rum
2	lemon slices
	sugar syrup

Prepare hot tea and add the rum, flamed in a tablespoon.

Add lemon slices and sugar to taste. Serve at once.

VIENNESE TEA

250 ml/1 cup	strong black tea
1 measure	dark rum
	sugar

Prepare strong fresh tea. Add sugar to taste and the rum. Serve hot.

BENGAL TIGER

1 tsp	lemon juice
2 dashes	aromatic bitters
½ tsp	sugar
45 g/1½ oz	cognac
125 ml/½ cup	strong black tea, cold

Mix lemon juice, sugar and bitters in a tall glass.

Fill with ice cubes and pour in the cognac then the tea.

Garnish with a lemon slice and sprig of mint.

RUM PUNCH

	juice of ½ lemon
1-1½ tsp	sugar
45 g/1½ oz	dark rum
	cracked ice
	iced tea
	sprigs of mint

Squeeze lemon juice into a highball glass. Add sugar and stir until dissolved. Fill the glass with cracked ice. Add rum and the tea and decorate with sprigs of mint.

ICED TEA PUNCH

(For 12)

2½ litres/10 cups	boiling water
3 tbsp	tea leaves
315 ml/1¼ cups	cognac
351 ml/1¼ cups	cointreau or grand marnier
2	oranges
	sugar

Infuse the tea leaves in boiling water and leave for 5 minutes. Pour into a punch bowl and leave to cool, then add plenty of ice cubes. Pour in the cognac and orange liqueur and add the orange separated into segments, and the peel removed in a spiral.

Stir in sugar to taste and serve while very cold.

JEWISH TEA PUNCH

625 ml/2½ cups	black China tea
125 ml/½ cup	claret
	juice of ½ lemon
	sugar to taste
3-4 slices	cucumber

Mix tea and claret, adding lemon juice and sugar to taste. Pour over cracked ice and garnish with cucumber. Serve while ice cold.

HOOGHLY HANGOVER

45 g/1½ oz	vodka
1 tsp	sugar
	juice of ½ lemon
60 g/2 oz	strong black tea, cold

Mix vodka with lemon juice and sugar in an old-fashioned glass.

Stir to dissolve. Fill with crushed ice and pour in the tea. Serve with mint.

As the myriad blends and widespread consumption figures prove, tea is available in almost every country of the world. As Britain's tea habits suggest, it can also be drunk at just about any time of the day and night. But the question of what type of tea to drink at what time of the day is one that distinguishes the addict from the connoisseur; and for any dedicated tea drinker, a little adventure into the established etiquette of tea drinking can only open up a whole new wealth of tastes and surprises.

According to Twinings, most British tea drinkers (85 percent) prefer pungent coloury tea from India or Ceylon, which is ideal for the early morning, breakfast time and all through the various "elevenses." A brisk tea, it should be used mainly as a morning wakeup beverage, though many people drink it all day long. But why not experiment a bit with the afternoon and evening hours? Darjeeling may be delicious after lunch, but China teas go down well at tea-time, along with Earl Grey, Orange Pekoe and Lemon. Indian and Ceylon teas may be best suited to high tea, but in the evening, after dinner, the peace and tranquillity of the day's end calls for the speciality blends — Earl Grey, Formosa oolong, Prince of Wales, Russian Caravan, Jasmine and Lapsang Souchong.

Among the various Twinings speciality blends, Indian teas break down into two retail categories, Assam and Darjeeling. The first, from the Assam region of northern India, produces a full-coloured liquor and is the traditional British cup of tea at its best. It's most widely drunk as the first cup of the day, and as a full-bodied beverage for afternoon tea. Darjeeling, from the Himalayan foothills, has a distinctive "muscatel" flavour, and is recommended as an after-dinner drink in place of coffee. It should be served in small to medium-sized cups, without milk or sugar. Try it also as a nightcap, with milk and sugar to taste.

Earl Grey, delicately scented and producing a pale clear liquor, is a fine connoisseur afternoon tea, best served with a slice of lemon or a drop of milk. Sugar is optional. It is excellent as an accompaniment to fish dishes, and gives a tasty "spike" of flavour when added to other teas. A spoonful of Earl Grey to three of Ceylon or Darjeeling makes for a much more distinguished pot. The Chinese Lapsang Souchong, produced in Fukien province and producing a pale liquor with a distinctive aroma and flavour, is an ideal drink — served without milk or sugar — at any time when you can relax and savour its very special taste. When served with Chinese and Japanese foods or any spicy dish, it should be offered on its own in small cups.

Lemon scented tea is a satisfying drink at any time of the day, especially in summer, and China's Keemun blend is best suited to the afternoon, served hot with a dash of milk but no sugar. This delicately flavoured tea, low in tannin, with a light-coloured liquor, also makes an excellent companion for Chinese food. Among the Ceylon blends, Uva, grown high on the hillsides of Sri Lanka, produces a gold-coloured liquor and a distinctive flowery bouquet. It can be served hot with milk and sugar at any time of the day, or as a relaxing evening drink.

But outside the speciality market, there's more to Indian and Ceylon teas than that. India, in particular, produces a wide variety of regional teas, most of them full-bodied, rich and malty, with leaf characteristics that differ according to the district in which they're grown.

Dooars: The leaf has a black appearance but the liquors are generally soft and mellow, very flowery and full-bodied. They are softer than Assams and less flavoury than Darjeelings but are much sought after for blending. As teas, they are a good compromise between Darjeeling flavour and Assam pungency.

Terai: The leaf is small and black and gives fair to good liquor approaching that of the Dooars.

Cachar: Produced in the Surma Valley of Assam, these teas have a leaf of greyish black appearance and the liquors are thick and sweet but generally less pungent than Assams.

Dehra Dun, Kumaon, Almora, Garhwal: These areas produce mostly green tea for trade with Tibet and Nepal. The leaf is small and close and liquors are light and brisk.

Kangra Valley: More green tea is produced here, with a peculiarly delicate and somewhat spicy flavour. They find a good market in Afghanistan, exported to there through Amritsar.

Ranchi: More green tea, mostly made from the China variety. The tea exhibits some body and strength and a slightly brassy-flavour.

South India produces tea very similar to that of Sri Lanka, due

to their geographical proximity. Main growing areas are situated on the slopes of the Western Ghats.

Anamallais: These teas possess good body and strength, somewhat similar to Travancore (Kerala) teas, but much stronger.

Nilgiris: These are high-grown teas produced on the Blue Mountain or Nilgiris. They present fine flavour with a brisk and pungent liquor.

Nilgiri-Wynaad: A fair tea comes from here, resembling the Travancore variety.

Malabar-Wynaad: Produces a low-grown tea, widely used as fillers.

Kerala: Generally, these are similar to Ceylon teas. They are flavoury in the cup with strength and have a fair leaf appearance. The High Range produces excellent quality teas and, being a high-grown variety, they're very flavoury.

South Travancore, Central Travancore (Peermade): These districts produce good and useful teas of medium grade, again much sought after as fillers.

Ceylon teas are produced in three main areas and graded under three categories: *Dimbula* — a typical high-grown tea from gardens 5,000 feet or more above sea level, with a fine flavour and golden colour; *Nuwara Eliya* (pronounced New-ray-lia) — a delicate tea famous for its light bright colour and fragrance; *Uva* — grown on the eastern slopes of the Central Mountains, has a fine flavour. The bright liquoring and distinctive teas from East and Central Africa are not retailed under their own names, and are substantially and increasingly used by blenders of the main brands of tea.

Indian and Ceylon teas can be found in any grocer's shop or supermarket in any country where tea is a beverage of any note. Teas can also be tasted, and retail orders presented, at Tea Board of India centres in the following capital cities: London, New York, Sydney, Cairo and Brussels. Sri Lanka has set up Ceylon Tea Centres in London, Glasgow, Manchester, Birmingham, Exeter and Leeds.

A list of teas, together with the 1983 prices, on sale in the India Tea Centre in London (343-349 Oxford Street, London W1R 1HB) is as follows:

1 lb Prestige caddy of Tata-Finlay (Darjeeling) £3

1 kg Runglee/Rungliot mini-chest of Birpara Tea Company Ltd (Darjeeling) £5

500 gram Animal/Bird caddy of TTCI (Darjeeling) £3.50

500 gram Rural Beauty caddy of TTCI (Darjeeling) £3

½ lb Maya caddy of TTCI (Finest Indian Tea) £1.45

25 Nataraj tea bags of TTCI £0.30

500 gram Jay Shree caddy (Darjeeling) £3

100 gram silverpot caddy of D.C. Ghose & Co. (Super Indian Tea) £0.85

¼ lb Darjeeling pack of Brooke Bond £0.45

¼ lb Assam pack of Brooke Bond £0.40

¼ lb Nilgiri pack of Brooke Bond £0.40

Choicest tea bags of Brooke Bond (100% Indian) £0.35

½ lb Darjeeling pack of Liptons £1.35

½ lb Assam pack of Liptons £1.20

½ lb Special Indian Blend of LTPC (Darjeeling) £1.40

½ lb Special Morning Blend of LTPC (Darjeeling) £1.15

1 lb Rich London Blend of LTPC (Darjeeling) £2.20

12 oz gift pack of LTPC £2.15

Oxfam Pack (Indian tea — Darjeeling, Assam & Nilgiri) £1.50

Outside the Indian Tea Centres, a selection of teas can also be ordered direct from the Indian manufacturers and British blenders.

Fortnum & Mason, at 181 Piccadilly, London W1A 1ER, offer the following wide variety of pure and blended teas and special packs (1978 prices):

PURE INDIA & CEYLON TEAS

Pure Darjeeling — F/M Broken Orange Pekoe Extra
 1 lb tin £2.80
 ½ lb tin £1.42½
 7 lb chest £19.75

Pure Darjeeling Flowery Orange Pekoe Extra
 1 lb tin £1.50
 ½ lb tin 77½p
 7 lb chest £10.50

Pure Darjeeling Broken Orange Pekoe
 1 lb tin £1.20
 ½ lb tin 62½p
 7 lb chest £8.55

Pure Darjeeling Superb
 1 lb packet 90p
 ½ lb packet 45p
 7 lb chest £6.45

Pure Assam Golden Broken Orange Pekoe
 1 lb tin £1.80
 ½ lb tin 92½p
 7 lb chest £12.75

Pure Assam Superb
 1 lb packet 90p
 ½ lb packet 45p
 7 lb chest £6.45

Pure Ceylon Specially Fine Broken Orange Pekoe
 1 lb tin £1.10
 ½ lb tin 57½p
 7 lb chest £7.55

Pure Ceylon Flowery Orange Pekoe Superb
 1 lb tin £1.00
 ½ lb tin 52½p
 7 lb chest £7.15

Pure Ceylon Broken Orange Pekoe
 1 lb packet 75p
 ½ lb packet 37½p
 7 lb chest £5.40

Orange Pekoe Blended Ceylon
 1 lb tin 90p
 ½ lb tin 47½p

BLENDED INDIA & CEYLON TEAS

Celebration	1 lb tin	85p
	½ lb tin	45p
	7 lb chest	£6.10
Royal	1 lb packet	75p
	½ lb packet	37½p
	7 lb chest	£5.40
Queen Anne	1 lb packet	70p
	½ lb packet	35p
	7 lb chest	£5.05
Old Silver Teapot	1 lb packet	65p
	½ lb packet	32½p
Perfection	1 lb packet	55p
	½ lb packet	27½p
Tea bags	carton of 25	20p

BLENDED INDIA & CHINA TEAS

Crown	1 lb tin	85p
	½ lb tin	45p
	7 lb chest	£6.10
Fortmason	1 lb tin	£1.00
	½ lb tin	52½p

PURE CHINA TEAS

Lapsang Souchong	1 lb packet	90p
	½ lb packet	45p
	7 lb chest	£6.45
Keemun	1 lb packet	80p
	½ lb packet	40p
	7 lb chest	£5.75
Earl Grey Blend	1 lb packet	75p
	½ lb packet	37½p
	7 lb chest	£5.40
Dowager Blend	1 lb tin	£1.00
	½ lb tin	52½p
Gunpowder Green	½ lb tin	57½p
Scented Orange Pekoe	½ lb tin	57½p
Mandarin Pekoe	1 lb tin	£1.00
	½ lb tin	52½p
Ichang	1 lb tin	£1.20
	½ lb tin	62½p
Jasmine with flowers	1 lb tin	£1.00
	½ lb tin	52½p
Formosa Oolong Superb	1 lb packet	£1.00
	½ lb packet	50p
	7 lb chest	£7.15
Oolong Leaf Bud	1 lb tin	£4.40
	½ lb tin	£2.20
	¼ lb tin	£1.10

All teas in packets are also available in 1 lb tins at
10p each extra or in ½ lb tins at 7½p extra.

GIFT BOXES OF TEA

Four ½ size green tins	$3.00
Six ¼ size green tins	$2.25
Four ½ size clock tins	$3.25
Six ½ size clock tins	$4.00

Teas contained in boxes of four —
Royal Blend, Darjeeling, Earl Grey Blend and
Lapsang Souchong.

Teas contained in boxes of six — Royal Blend,
Ceylon, Darjeeling, Earl Grey Blend,
Lapsang Souchong and Jasmine.

DECORATED JARS OF TEA

Designs exclusive to Fortnum & Mason.
Hand-enamelled on Staffordshire ironstone.

½ lb size filled with Royal Blend or Lapsang Souchong	$2.50
1 lb jars	$4.50

Wedgwood jars and Coalport jars of tea
specially made for Fortnum & Mason.

½ lb size filled Royal Blend or Lapsang Souchong	$6.50
Blue Ascot Teapot filled ½ lb. Royal Blend Tea	$3.00
Brocade Teapot	$4.50
Heat Resisting Glass Teapots with Infuser	$3.25
Coalport White Cabbage Teapots	$4.50 & $5.50
English Tea Cosies	$2.50

TISANES

YERBA MATE, The South American Tonic
27½p per ½ lb and 1 lb tins 50p

ASSAMBA FILTRA

**Tisanes packed in Switzerland and specially
imported direct by Fortnum and Mason
in cartons containing 20 tea-bags.**

LIME FLOWERS, for headaches and sleeplessness, per carton	27½p
CHAMOMILE FLOWERS, an excellent tonic	27½p
PEPPERMINT, for indigestion	27½p
ROSE HIPS & HIBISCUS FLOWERS, rich in Vitamin C	29½p

Jacksons of Piccadilly also offer a wide variety of fine teas, leaded of course by their original Earl Grey's blend — a delicately scented tea with mild flavour. Other blends retailing in London and exported around the world are:

English Breakfast
This tea is made from the small leaf teas of India & Ceylon. It makes a rich strong brew and is therefore very popular at the breakfast table.

Ceylon Orange Pekoe
This tea has a black medium sized leaf which makes an exceptionally strong liquor of full flavour.

Darjeeling
Harvested from the hills of Darjeeling, this large leaf variety is the finest and most distinctive of Indian Teas.

Coronation Tea
Is a perfect blend of teas combining the character of Ceylon tea with the strength of Indian tea. This blend was specially prepared in the early summer of 1953 to commemorate the Coronation of H. M. Queen Elizabeth II.

Jasmine Blossom
A delicate tea mixed with Jasmine flowers, which give a flavour and bouquet of oriental mystery.

Lady Londonderry's Mixture
A blend of Ceylon, India and Formosa teas used by London's famous social and political hostess of the first half of this century.

Lapsang Souchong
A long-leaf Formosan tea with the distinctive tarry flavour produced by slow firing over wood smoke while it is drying in the sun. Best drunk without milk and with a slice of lemon.

Formosa Oolong
A tea with a large bold leaf, but with a delicate and soft peach-like flavour. The seed, which originally came from Indo-China, produces an unusually small bush, which yields a light but high quality crop.

Ching Wo
This delicately scented tea is not often seen outside China. It is grown deep in the province of Fukien, where few Europeans have ever penetrated. Connoisseurs of the exotic East will particularly appreciate Ching Wo tea, which is best drunk with a slice of lemon.

Assam Tea
A very strong tea grown in the north east corner of Assam, through which flows the Brahmaputra river. On the one side we get the delicate Darjeeling tea and, on the other, the full-bodied tea of Assam. This blend contains an unusually high proportion of best quality tips.

Lemon Tea
A unique blend of Ceylon teas, mixed with lemon peel and scented with lemon essence. It should be served either hot or iced, without milk. Sugar brings out the delicious lemon flavour.

Russian Tea
This tea is grown in the foothills of the Caucasian mountains near the border between Russia and Turkey. It is long leafed and has a character and appearance not unlike some of the teas from China. It is best drunk with a slice of lemon.

Jackson's 'Victorian' Tea Caddies
This recently introduced range of attractive caddies, based upon an original Victorian design, consists of four caddies, all containing Jackson's Teas.

1 Plum-coloured caddy filled with ½lb of Earl Grey's tea.

2 Dark green caddy filled with ½lb of Breakfast tea.

3 Blue caddy filled with ½lb of Evening Tea (a blend of Ceylon, Indian and Formosan teas).

4 Mauve caddy, filled with ½lb of Afternoon Tea (a blend of Indian and Ceylon teas).

In the United Kingdom Jackson's teas are sold in leading department stores and quality food shops. They are, of course, also obtainable in Jackson's own shops.

In London at:
171/172 Piccadilly, London W1V 0LL

6a/6b Sloane Street and 1 Basil Street, London SW1X 9LE

24 Kendal Street, Hyde Park, London W2 2AE

In Bournemouth at:
37-41 Seamoor Road Bournemouth, Hampshire

In Tunbridge Wells at:
37 Mount Ephraim Tunbridge Wells, Kent

In St Albans at:
Thos. Oakley
9 George Street St Albans, Hertfordshire

In Hitchin at:
Halsey & Sons Market Place, Hitchin, Hertfordshire

Jacksons of Piccadilly teas are also available in more than 30 countries, and in cities as diverse as Reykjavik in Iceland, Dubai on the Persian Gulf, Melbourne in Australia, Hong Kong, Tokyo and San Francisco.

Some well known department and quality stores selling Jackson's Teas:
Austria, Julius Meinl AG
Canada, T. Eaton & Co.
Denmark, Magazin du Nord
France, Fauchon and Hediard
Holland, Vroom & Dreesmann
Italy, La Rinascente
Japan, Mitsukoshi, Daimaru, Matsuya, Matsuzakaya and Takashimaya
South Africa, Stuttafords
Sweden, Arvid Nordquist, Ahlens
USA, Bloomingdales, Marshall Field, Neiman Marcus
The United Kingdom, Most leading department stores and quality food shops

China teas are becoming increasingly available in Western supermarkets, Chinese food and produce stores and department stores opened up directly by the People's Republic of China as outlets for its foods and manufactures. Alternatively, gift parcels of selected teas can be ordered by mail from the China Tea Company in Hong Kong — write to them c/o GPO Box 5680, Hong Kong, and they'll send back the following gift parcel list with the latest prices in Hong Kong dollars for both the USA and British markets, and any other country you care to mention.

Parcel No.	Contents	Net weight
	China Black Tea Parcel	
No. 1	2 tins Lion Mountain Black Tea	2 lbs
No. 2	2 tins Peony Brand Keemun Tea	2 lbs
No. 3	2 tins Flower Basket Bd. Keemun Tea	2 lbs
No. 4	2 tins Peacock Brand Keemun Tea	2 lbs
No. 5	2 tins Lapsang Souchong Tea	2 lbs
No. 6	4 tins Lion Mountain Black Tea	4 lbs
No. 7	4 tins Peony Brand Keemun Tea	4 lbs
No. 8	4 tins Flower Basket Bd. Keemun Tea	4 lbs
No. 9	4 tins Peacock Brand Keemun Tea	4 lbs
No. 10	4 tins Lapsang Souchong Tea	4 lbs
	China Green Tea Parcel	
No. 11	2 tins Extra Choicest Jasmine Tea	2 lbs
No. 12	2 tins Scented Jasmine Tea	2 lbs
No. 13	2 tins Extra Choicest Tit Koon Yum Tea	1½ lbs
No. 14	2 tins Tit Koon Yum Tea	1½ lbs
No. 15	2 tins Sui Sin Tea	1½ lbs
No. 16	4 tins Extra Choicest Jasmine Tea	4 lbs
No. 17	4 tins Scented Jasmine Tea	4 lbs
No. 18	4 tins Extra Choicest Tit Koon Yum Tea	3 lbs
No. 19	4 tins Tit Koon Yum Tea	3 lbs
No. 20	4 tins Sui Sin Tea	3 lbs
	China Black & Green Tea Parcel	
No. 21	1 tin Peony Brand Keemun Tea	1 lb
	1 tin Scented Jasmine Tea	1 lb
No. 22	1 tin Flower Basket Bd. Keemun Tea	1 lb
	1 tin Scented Jasmine Tea	1 lb
No. 23	1 tin Peony Brand Keemun Tea	1 lb
	1 tin Tit Koon Yum Tea	12 oz
No. 24	1 tin Flower Basket Bd. Keemum Tea	1 lb
	1 tin Tit Koon Yum Tea	12 oz
No. 25	1 tin Peony Brand Keemun Tea	1 lb
	1 tin Sui Sin Tea	12 oz
No. 26	1 tin Flower Basket Bd. Keemun Tea	1 lb
	1 tin Sui Sin Tea	12 oz
No. 27	2 tins Peony Brand Keemun Tea	2 lbs
	2 tins Scented Jasmine Tea	2 lbs
No. 28	2 tins Flower Basket Bd. Keemun Tea	2 lbs
	2 tins Scented Jasmine Tea	2 lbs
No. 29	2 tins Peony Brand Keemun Tea	2 lbs
	2 tins Tit Koon Yum Tea	1½ lbs

Parcel No.	Contents	Net weight
	China Black & Green Tea Parcel	
No. 30	2 tins Flower Basket Bd. Keemun Tea	2 lbs
	2 tins Tit Koon Yum Tea	1½ lbs
No. 31	2 tins Peony Brand Keemun Tea	2 lbs
	2 tins Sui Sin Tea	1½ lbs
No. 32	2 tins Flower Basket Bd. Keemun Tea	2 lbs
	2 tins Sui Sin Tea	1½ lbs
	Ginger Parcel	
No. 33	2 tins Preserved Ginger	2 lbs
No. 34	4 tins Preserved Ginger	4 lbs
No. 35	2 tins Stem Ginger in Syrup	3 lbs
No. 36	3 tins Stem Ginger in Syrup	4½ lbs
	Black Tea & Ginger Parcel	
No. 37	1 tin Peony Brand Keemun Tea	1 lb
	1 tin Preserved Ginger	1 lb
No. 38	1 tin Flower Basket Bd. Keemun Tea	1 lb
	1 tin Preserved Ginger	1 lb
No. 39	2 tins Peony Brand Keemun Tea	2 lbs
	2 tins Preserved Ginger	2 lbs
No. 40	2 tins Flower Basket Bd. Keemun Tea	2 lbs
	2 tins Preserved Ginger	2 lbs
	Green Tea & Ginger Parcel	
No. 41	1 tin Extra Choicest Jasmine Tea	1 lb
	1 tin Preserved Ginger	1 lb
No. 42	1 tin Scented Jasmine Tea	1 lb
	1 tin Preserved Ginger	1 lb
No. 43	2 tins Extra Choicest Jasmine Tea	2 lbs
	2 tins Preserved Ginger	2 lbs
No. 44	2 tins Scented Jasmine Tea	2 lbs
	2 tins Preserved Ginger	2 lbs
	Small Packet Tea Parcel	
No. 45	1 tin Lion Mountain Keemun Tea	1 lb
No. 46	1 tin Peony Brand Keemun Tea	1 lb
No. 47	1 tin Flower Basket Bd. Keemun Tea	1 lb
No. 48	1 tin Lapsang Souchong Tea	1 lb
No. 49	1 tin Extra Choicest Jasmine Tea	1 lb
No. 50	1 tin Scented Jasmine Tea	1 lb
No. 51	1 tin Tit Koon Yum Tea	12 oz
No. 52	1 tin Sui Sin Tea	12 oz

BIBLIOGRAPHY

The Book of Coffee & Tea, Joel, David & Karl Schapira, 1974, St Martin's Press, N.Y.

Teacraft, Charles & Violet Schafer, 1975, Yerba Buena Press, San Francisco.

The Peninsula Magazine, Robin Moyer, August 1978.

Tea for the British, Denys Forrest, 1973, Chatto & Windus Ltd, London.

Two Hundred and Fifty Years of Tea and Coffee, Stephen H. Twining, 1956, R. Twining & Co. Ltd., London.

The Classic of Tea, Lu Yu (Francis Ross Carpenter), 1974, Little, Brown & Company.

Off-Duty, Michele Kay, Pacific Edition, January 1978.

Tea Gardens of the World, John H. Blake, 1902.

America, Alistair Cooke, 1973, Alfred A. Knopf Inc., N.Y.

A History of Hong Kong, G.B. Endacott, 1964, Oxford University Press.

Gemini News Service, Cecil Porter.

Modern Asia, Shirley Payoe, June 1978.

Asia Yearbook, The Far Eastern Economic Review, Hong Kong.

Late Georgian and Regency Silver, Judith Banister, Country Life Collectors' Guides.

Wild Coffee & Tea Substitutes of Canada, Nancy J. Turner & Adam F. Szczawinski, The National Museum of Natural Sciences.

Cosmopolitan Magazine, Carole Getzoff.

Feed Your Face, Dian Dincin Buchman, 1973, Gerald Duckworth & Co. Ltd., London.

Tea Leaf Reading, Kathleen McCormack, Collins.

ACKNOWLEDGEMENTS

References in the text denote quotations from the following source publications:

Chapter 2
The Story of Tea — 1, 2, 7, 8, 11, 20, 23, 25, 31
Teacraft — 3, 13, 17, 19, 29, 33, 39, 41, 43
Peninsula Magazine — 4, 40
Sir Percival Griffiths — 5
Tea for the British — 6, 9, 10, 15, 26, 27, 28, 30, 32, 35, 36, 38
Two Hundred and Fifty Years of Tea and Coffee — 12
A Brief History of Tea, Jacksons of Piccadilly — 14, 16, 18, 21
Off-Duty — 22
Tea Gardens of the World — 24, 42
America — 34
A History of Hong Kong — 37
Gemini News Service — 4

Chapter 3
Tea for the British — 1, 2, 5
Two Hundred and Fifty Years of Tea and Coffee — 3
Tea Gardens of the World — 4, 9
The Story of Tea — 6
Modern Asia — 7
How Ceylon Tea is Grown and Marketed — 8
The Asia Yearbook — 10

Chapter 4
Tea for the British — 1, 7, 10, 12
Tea Gardens of the World — 2
Teacraft — 3, 4, 11, 18
Peninsula Magazine — 5, 6
Late Georgian and Regency Silver — 8, 9
Wild Coffee & Tea Substitutes of Canada — 13
Cosmopolitan — 14
Feed Your Face — 15
Tea Leaf Reading — 16
The Story of Tea and Coffee — 17

Chapter 5
Teacraft — 1, 2

PICTURE CREDITS

115.

101098

茶經三卷唐陸羽撰羽字鴻漸一名疾字季疵號桑苧翁復州竟陵人上元初隱於苕溪徵拜太子文學又徙太常寺太祝並不就職貞元初卒事迹具唐書隱逸傳稱羽嗜茶著經三篇藝文志載之小說家作三卷與今本同陳師道後山集有茶經序曰陸羽茶經家書一卷畢氏王氏書三卷張氏書四卷內外書十有一卷其文繁簡不同王畢氏書繁雜意其舊本張書簡明與家書合而多脫誤

一之源　二之具　三之造　四之器　五之煮
六之飲　七之事　八之出　九之略　十之圖

一之源

茶者南方之嘉木也一尺二尺迺至數十尺其巴山峽川有兩人合抱者伐而掇之其樹如瓜蘆葉如梔子花如白薔薇實如栟櫚莖如丁香根如胡桃其字或從草或從木或草木幷其名一曰茶二曰檟三曰蔎四曰茗五曰荈其地上者生爛石中者生礫壤下者生黃土凡藝而不實植而罕茂法如種瓜三歲可採野者上園者次陽崖陰林紫者上綠者次筍者上芽者次葉卷上葉舒次

陰山坡谷者不堪採掇性凝滯結瘕疾茶之爲用味至寒爲飲最宜精行儉德之人若熱渴凝悶腦疼目澀四支煩百節不舒聊四五啜與醍醐甘露抗衡也採不時造不精雜以卉莽飲之成疾茶爲累也亦猶人參上者生上黨中者生百濟新羅下者生高麗有生澤州易州幽州檀州者爲藥無效況非此者設服薺苨使六疾不瘳知人參爲累則茶累盡矣

二之具

籝一曰籃一曰籠一曰筥以竹織之受五升或一斗二斗三斗者茶人負以採茶也

竈無用突者釜用脣口者

承一曰臺一曰砧以石爲之不然以槐桑木半埋地中遣無所搖動

檐一曰衣以油絹或雨衫單服敗者爲之以檐置承上又以規置檐上以造茶也茶成舉而易之

芘莉一曰羸子一曰篣筤以二小竹長三尺軀亦二赤五寸柄五寸以篾織方眼如圃人土羅闊二尺以列茶也（赤闕尺闕）

棨一曰錐刀柄以堅木爲之用穿茶也

撲一曰鞭以竹爲之穿茶以解茶也

焙鑿地深二尺闊二尺五寸長一丈上作短牆高二尺泥之

貫削竹爲之長二尺五寸以貫焙茶也

棚一曰棧以木構于焙上編木兩層高一尺以焙茶也茶之半乾昇下棚全乾昇上棚

穿（音釧）江東淮南剖竹爲之巴川峽山紉穀皮爲之江東以一斤爲上穿半斤爲中穿四兩五兩爲小穿峽中以一百二十斤爲上穿八十斤爲中穿五十斤爲小穿字舊作釵釧之釧字或作貫串今則不然如磨扇彈鑽縫五字文以平聲書之義以去聲呼之其字以穿

紙囊

紙囊以剡藤紙白厚者夾縫之以貯所炙茶使不泄其香也

碾（拂末）

碾以橘木爲之次以梨桑桐柘爲之內圓而外方內圓備于運行也外方制其傾危也內容墮而外無餘木墮形如車輪不輻而軸焉長九寸闊一寸七分墮徑三寸八分中厚一寸邊厚半寸軸中方而執圓其拂末以鳥羽製之

羅合

羅末以合蓋貯之以則置合中用巨竹剖而屈之以紗絹衣之其合以竹節爲之或屈杉以漆之高三寸蓋一寸底二寸口徑四寸

則

則以海貝蠣蛤之屬或以銅鐵竹匕策之類則者量也准也度也凡煮水一升用末方寸匕若好薄者減之嗜濃者增之故云則也

水方

水方以椆木槐楸梓等合之其裏幷外縫漆之受一斗

漉水囊

漉水囊若常用者其格以生銅鑄之以備水濕無有苔穢腥澀意以熟銅苔穢鐵腥澀也林棲谷隱者或用之竹木木與竹非持久涉遠之具故用之生銅爲囊織青竹以捲之裁碧縑以縫之紐翠鈿以綴之又作綠油囊以貯之圓徑五寸柄一寸五分

瓢

瓢一曰犧杓剖瓠爲之或刊木爲之晉舍人杜毓荈賦云酌之以匏匏瓢也口闊脛薄柄短永嘉中餘姚人虞洪入瀑布山採茗遇一道士云吾丹丘子祈子他日甌犧之餘乞相遺也犧木杓也今常用以梨木爲之

竹筴

竹筴或以桃柳蒲葵木爲之或以柿心木爲之長一尺銀裹兩頭

鹺簋（揭）

鹺簋以瓷爲之圓徑四寸若合形或瓶或罍貯鹽花也其揭竹製長四寸一分闊九分揭策也

熟盂

熟盂以貯熱水或瓷或沙受二升

盌

盌越州上鼎州次婺州次岳州次壽州洪州次或者以邢州處越州上殊爲不然若邢瓷類銀越瓷類玉邢不如越一也若邢瓷類雪則越瓷類冰邢不如越二也邢瓷白而茶色丹越瓷青而茶色綠邢不如越三也晉杜毓荈賦所謂器擇陶揀出自東甌甌越也甌越州上口脣不卷底卷而淺受半升已下越州瓷岳瓷皆青青則益茶茶作紅白之色邢州瓷白茶色紅壽州瓷黃茶色紫洪州瓷褐茶色黑悉不宜茶

畚

畚以白蒲卷而編之可貯盌十枚或用筥其紙帊以剡紙夾縫令方亦十之也

札

札緝栟櫚皮以茱萸木夾而縛之或截竹束而管之若巨筆形

滌方

滌方以貯滌洗之餘用楸木合之制如水方受八升

滓方

三盌至七行五盌若六人已下不約盌數但闕一人而已其雋永補所闕人

七之事

三皇炎帝神農氏周魯周公旦齊相晏嬰漢仙人丹丘子黃山君司馬文園令相如揚執戟雄吳歸命侯韋太傅弘嗣晉惠帝劉司空琨琨兄子兗州刺史演張黃門孟陽傅司隸咸江洗馬統孫參軍楚左記室太沖陸吳興納納兄子會稽內史俶謝冠軍安石郭弘農璞桓揚州溫杜舍人毓武康小山寺釋法瑤沛國夏侯愷餘姚虞洪北地傅巽丹陽弘君舉高安任育長宣城秦精敦煌單道開剡縣陳務妻廣陵老姥河內山謙之後魏瑯琊王肅宋新安王子鸞鸞弟豫章王子尚鮑照妹令暉八公山沙門譚濟齊世祖武帝梁劉廷尉陶先生弘景皇朝徐英公勣

神農食經茶茗久服令人有力悅志

周公爾雅檟苦荼廣雅云荊巴間採葉作餅葉老者餅成以米膏出之欲煮茗飲先炙令赤色搗末置瓷器中以湯澆覆之用葱薑橘子芼之其飲醒酒令人不眠

晏子春秋嬰相齊景公時食脫粟之飯炙三戈五卵茗菜而已

司馬相如凡將篇烏喙桔梗芫華款冬貝母木蘗蔞芩草芍藥桂漏蘆蜚廉雚菌荈詫白斂白芷菖蒲芒消莞椒茱萸

方言蜀西南人謂茶曰蔎

吳志韋曜傳孫皓每饗宴坐席無不率以七升爲限雖不盡入口皆澆灌取盡曜飲酒不過二升皓初禮異密賜茶荈以代酒

晉中興書陸納爲吳興太守時衛將軍謝安欲詣納納兄子俶怪納無所備不敢問之乃私蓄十數人饌安既至所設惟茶果而已俶遂陳盛饌珍羞必具及安去納杖俶四十云汝既不能光益叔父奈何穢吾素業

晉書桓溫爲揚州牧性儉每讌飲唯下七奠柈茶果而已

搜神記夏侯愷因疾死宗人字狗奴察見鬼神見愷來收馬幷病其妻見著平上幘單衣入坐生時西壁大床就人覓茶飲

劉琨與兄子南兗州刺史演書云前得安州乾薑一斤黃芩一斤桂一斤皆所須也吾體中憒悶常仰真茶汝可置也

傅咸司隸教曰聞南方有以困蜀嫗作茶粥賣爲廉事打破其器具又賣餅于市而禁茶粥以蜀嫗何哉

神異記餘姚人虞洪入山採茗遇一道士牽三青牛引洪至瀑布山曰吾丹丘子也聞子善具飲常思見惠山中有大茗可以相給祈子他日有甌犧之餘乞相遺也因立奠祀後常令家人入山獲大茗焉

左思嬌女詩吾家有嬌女皎皎頗白皙小字爲紈素口齒自清歷有姊字蕙芳眉目粲如畫馳騖翔園林果下皆生摘貪華風雨中倏忽數百適心爲茶荈劇吹噓對鼎䥶

張孟陽登成都樓詩云借問揚子舍想見長卿廬程卓累千金驕侈擬五侯門有連騎客翠帶腰吳鉤鼎食隨時進百和妙且殊披林採秋橘臨江釣春魚黑子過龍醢果饌踰蟹蝑芳茶冠六情溢味播九區人生苟安樂茲土聊可娛

傅巽七誨蒲桃宛柰齊柿燕栗恒陽黃梨巫山朱橘南中茶子西極石蜜

弘君舉食檄寒溫既畢應下霜華之茗三爵而終應下諸蔗木瓜元李楊梅五味橄欖懸豹葵羹各一杯

孫楚歌茱萸出芳樹顛鯉魚出洛水泉白鹽出河東美豉出魯淵薑桂茶荈出巴蜀椒橘木蘭出高山蓼蘇出溝渠精稗出中田

華佗食論苦茶久食益意思

本草菜部苦茶一名荼一名選一名游冬生益州川谷山陵道傍凌冬不死三月三日採乾註云疑此即是今茶一名茶令人不眠

本草註按詩云誰謂荼苦又云堇荼如飴皆苦菜也陶謂之苦茶木類非菜流茗春採之謂之苦搽

枕中方療積年瘻苦茶蜈蚣並炙令香熟等分搗篩煮甘草湯洗以末傅之

孺子方療小兒無故驚蹶以苦茶葱鬚煮服之

八之出

山南以峽州上　襄州荊州次
衡州下　金州梁州又下
淮南以光州上　義陽郡舒州次
壽州下　蘄州黃州又下
浙西以湖州上　常州次
宣州杭州睦州歙州下　潤州蘇州又下
劍南以彭州上　綿州蜀州次
邛州次雅州瀘州下　眉州漢州又下
浙東以越州上　明州婺州次
台州下

黔中生恩州播州費州夷州江南生鄂州袁州吉州嶺南生福州建州韶州象州其恩播費夷鄂袁吉福建泉韶象十一州未詳往往得之其味極佳

九之略

其造具若方春禁火之時于野寺山園叢手而掇乃蒸乃舂乃復以火乾之則之棨撲焙貫棚穿育等七事皆廢其煮器若松間石上可坐則具列廢用槁薪鼎䥶之屬則風爐灰承炭檛火筴交床等廢若瞰泉臨澗則水方滌方漉水囊廢若五人以下茶可末而精者則羅合廢若援藟躋嵓引絙入洞于山口炙而末之或紙包合貯則碾拂末等廢既瓢盌筴札熟盂鹺簋悉以一筥盛之則都籃廢但城邑之中王公之門二十四器闕一則茶廢矣

十之圖

以絹素或四幅或六幅分布寫之陳諸座隅則茶之源之具之造之器之煮之飲之事之出之略目擊而存于是茶經之始終備焉

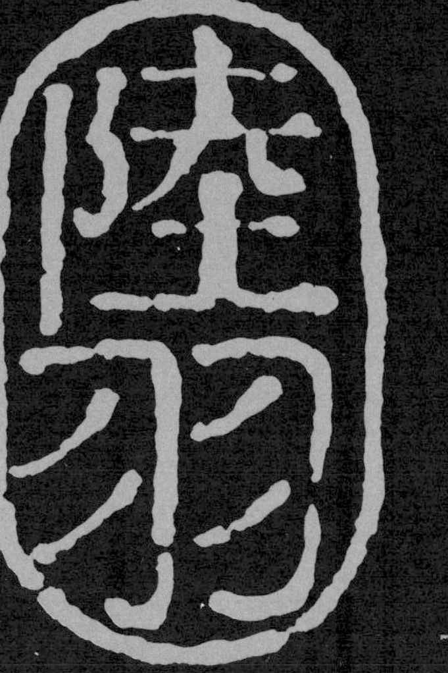